2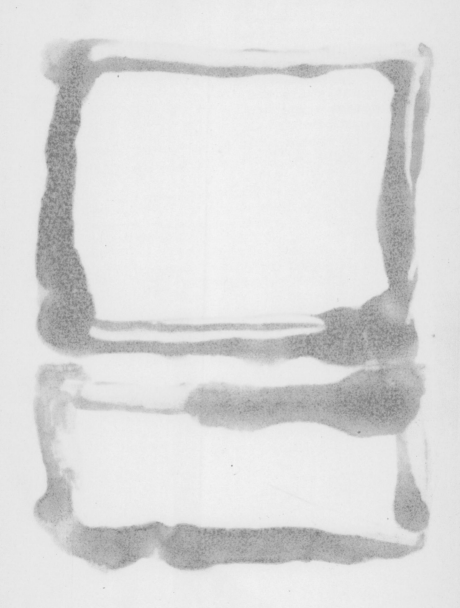

THE
GOSPEL MESSAGE
OF ST. MARK

THE
GOSPEL MESSAGE
OF ST. MARK

BY

R. H. LIGHTFOOT

OXFORD
AT THE CLARENDON PRESS
1950

Oxford University Press, Amen House, London E.C. 4

GLASGOW NEW YORK TORONTO MELBOURNE WELLINGTON
BOMBAY CALCUTTA MADRAS CAPE TOWN

Geoffrey Cumberlege, Publisher to the University

PRINTED IN GREAT BRITAIN

PREFACE

THE first four chapters of this book consist of four lectures delivered in October 1949 at the University College of South Wales and Monmouthshire. Of the remaining chapters, in the fifth I am much indebted to an article in *Theologische Blätter*, Oct.–Nov. 1941, very few copies of which are likely to have reached this country. Its author was Professor Ernst Lohmeyer of Greifswald, whose permission to draw upon his work in this way I have not been able to obtain, since to the deep regret of his friends and indeed of all New Testament students his present address, as a prisoner in eastern Europe, is unknown. I have, however, long had the privilege of his acquaintance and have every reason to believe that he would gladly allow his views to be laid before English readers in this way. The sixth and, in a modified form, the eighth chapters were originally written, at the request of the Editor of the *Expository Times*, for publication in that journal, and I am grateful for permission to reproduce them here, with some minor alterations and additions. The seventh chapter, in a shorter form, has been read to more than one society. I hope that the contents of the sixth and eighth chapters will be thought to bear closely enough on the themes of the rest of the book to justify their inclusion in it.

I realize that in a composite book of this sort there are certain repetitions. But I do not think that this is altogether a matter for regret, and therefore I have not tried entirely to excise them; and I hope that in this matter critics will not find ground for offence.

OXFORD

R. H. L.

December 1949

CONTENTS

I

THE RECEPTION OF ST. MARK'S GOSPEL
IN THE CHURCH AND A SURVEY OF ITS
CONTENTS

AMONG students of the New Testament, the Gospel according to St. Mark has aroused more interest in the last century than at any other time, so far as we can judge, since it was first put forth. This is such a remarkable fact that it is worth while to dwell upon it. It will have been noticed that I qualified my statement by the words 'so far as we can judge'. This is because we know very little indeed about the reception of St. Mark's gospel in the Church until the last half of the second century A.D. As regards the place and date of its production, there is much to be said for the view that it may have first seen the light at Rome towards the end of the life of Nero, who was emperor from A.D. 54 to 68. For the present at any rate let us assume, as a working hypothesis, that the place of writing was Rome, and the time between A.D. 65 and 70.

Unfortunately the allusions to, or quotations from, the gospels in Christian writings before the middle of the second century are very few, and this is more especially true of our second gospel. It might indeed have been thought, in Dr. Swete's words, that 'a work which was ascribed by contemporaries to a disciple and interpreter of St. Peter, and believed to consist of carefully registered reminiscences' of this apostle's teaching, would 'find a prompt and wide circulation in Christian communities, especially at Rome and in the West, where it is said to have been written'.* But, as Dr. Swete goes on to show, the letter addressed to the church of Corinth by Clement of Rome about A.D. 95 contains no certain reference to the book, and the same may be said, apart from two slight and perhaps doubtful exceptions, of all other writings which can certainly be dated before A.D. 150. Soon after this time, indeed, not only do we find definite traces of the use of this gospel, but from the last quarter, if not from the third quarter, of the second century,

* *The Gospel according to St. Mark*, 2nd. ed., p. xxix.

the four gospels, as is well known, were universally accepted in the Church.

None the less, St. Mark's gospel continued to suffer from relative neglect. Dr. Swete goes on to point out that no commentary upon it is known before that of a writer of the fifth or more probably of the sixth century, known as Victor of Antioch, who himself remarks that a careful inquiry had failed to reveal any predecessors in this task.* The next commentator on St. Mark known to us is our own countryman, the venerable Bede, in the eighth century; and finally Euthymius Zigabenus, a monk of Constantinople early in the twelfth century, though he writes on this gospel, scarcely regards it as deserving a separate commentary, for, as he says, 'the second gospel is in close agreement with the first, excepting where the first is fuller'. And these words give us at any rate a partial explanation of the comparative neglect of Mark throughout the centuries; his work has suffered through comparison with that of St. Matthew.

In the first place, Matthew was believed to be the work of an apostle; Mark was not.† Secondly, Matthew is almost twice the length of Mark, which contains very little indeed that is not found in Matthew also. Mark, in the English Revised Version, from 1^1 to 16^8, contains 666 verses; of these only some 50 verses find no parallel in Matthew. Thirdly, for the purpose of practical use Matthew must have proved far superior to Mark. For example, in all three synoptic gospels there are traces of arrangement of the material in the interests, possibly, of oral teaching or at least of easy retention in the memory; and this feature, which reaches its fullest development in Matthew, is very much less obvious in Mark. Fourthly, I will venture to express a personal belief, which grows steadily stronger, though I must not stop to try to justify it now, since it would lead us too far from our present subject. I suggest that the Person and portrait

---

* Professor G. D. Kilpatrick points out to me that Dr. Swete has failed to mention a patristic commentary on Mark, which may be of the first half of the fifth century; it may be found in Migne, *Pat. Lat.* xxx. 589 ff., where it is wrongly ascribed to St. Jerome. An interesting feature is that it usually has the vulgate text, but the commentary is clearly not always based upon that text.

† So far as possible, the expressions St. Matthew, St. Mark, &c., are used where the reference is to the evangelists themselves, and Matthew, Mark, &c. where the reference is to the books.

of the Lord, as offered for our reverent contemplation and worship in Matthew, is likely to be more intelligible and attractive to catholic churchmen, when we recall their devotion to law and order and precise definition, than the Person and the portrait, deeply human it is true, but also profoundly mysterious and baffling, in the pages of Mark. Fifthly and lastly, from at least the time of Irenaeus about A.D. 180, Mark was believed to have been written after Matthew; the prevailing view in the early centuries is expressed in some well-known words of St. Augustine, 'Marcus Matthaei tanquam breviator et pedisequus'.*

In any case, it is certain that throughout the centuries Matthew has been the most popular gospel of the four; and of the three remaining gospels, for the reasons set out above, none has stood to suffer so much from the fact of Matthew's popularity as Mark—a rather paradoxical fact, when we reflect that, so far from St. Mark being the abbreviator and follower of St. Matthew, St. Matthew, as we now have every reason to believe, is most deeply indebted to his great predecessor St. Mark.

Dr. Swete points out that this relatively inferior estimate in which the second gospel was held is found confirmed, if we study the order in which the gospels are placed in catalogues and manuscripts. The two principal groupings are these: (1) Matthew, Mark, Luke, John; (2) Matthew, John, Luke, Mark. The first grouping, which finally prevailed everywhere and to which we ourselves are accustomed, arranges the four gospels according to the order in which they were generally believed to have been written. The second grouping, which at first prevailed in the western churches, gives the place of honour to the two gospels which were believed to be the work of apostles, and places after them those gospels which were believed to be the work of followers of apostles. For our present purpose the relative inferiority of Mark in both lists is apparent; in the first group he comes next after Matthew as his abbreviator and follower; and in the second group he is preceded not only by Matthew and John but also (apart from two exceptions) by Luke.

Finally the comparative neglect or, it may be, the lack of

* 'Mark, as it were the abbreviator and follower of Matthew.'

comprehension of the early Church in respect of Mark may perhaps be illustrated in the distribution of the evangelical symbols among the four evangelists. From the last quarter of the second century A.D., the four gospels have been associated in Christian thought with the four Cherubim of the book of Ezekiel, and the corresponding four living creatures of the book of Revelation. In an often-quoted passage St. Irenaeus, maintaining that the gospels cannot be either more or fewer in number than four, applies to them severally the characteristics of the four living creatures of the Apocalypse. These four aspects of the living creatures, he says, represent the fourfold manner of operation of the Eternal Word. The lion symbolizes the royal office, the sovereign authority, and the effectual power of the son of God; the calf signifies His sacrificial and priestly character; the human face corresponds to His coming in human nature; and the flying eagle recalls the gift of the Spirit descending on His Church. Dr. Swete has shown that, although ancient writers, it is true, differ widely in their distribution of the symbols among the four evangelists, yet this diversity is seen at its greatest when they are dealing with St. Mark; in a list of four writers drawn up by Dr. Swete, to St. Mark and to St. Mark only among the four evangelists is assigned every one of the four symbols; thus to St. Irenaeus St. Mark represents the eagle, to St. Augustine the man, in a *Synopsis* wrongly ascribed to St. Athanasius he is the calf, and in the distribution favoured by St. Jerome he is the lion.

This phenomenon strikingly illustrates either the comparative neglect or at any rate the uncertainty and hesitation of the Church in estimating the place and function of our second gospel.*

At the present time, as I have remarked, the interest in the second gospel is at least as great as, perhaps even greater than the interest shown in any other. What are the causes of this remarkable change? May we not sum them up in a single phrase, the recent growth among us, for better, for worse, of the scientific or critical spirit?

* It is noticeable also that the number of quotations from Mark in the extant writings of such patristic authorities as St. Irenaeus, Clement of Alexandria, St. Cyprian, and St. Augustine is, even when we have made allowance for the comparative brevity of this gospel, very much smaller than the number made by them from the other three gospels.

Let us recall the reasons which may have helped to commend Matthew to the special regard of the early Church and may have led to a corresponding comparative neglect of Mark.

First, Matthew was believed to be the work of an apostle; Mark was not. But to-day very few of us are able to believe that Matthew as we have it is the work of the apostle St. Matthew.

Secondly, Matthew is much longer than Mark, and contains nearly everything that is found in Mark. This important fact of course remains, but to-day it does not lead to a neglect of Mark, especially as, in the little stories related in both Matthew and Mark, Mark is almost invariably the fuller and the more original and lifelike.

The third reason was the symmetry and admirable arrangement of Matthew. But to us this suggests literary reflection and editorial arrangement, and we turn all the more eagerly to the greater simplicity and incoherence of Mark, these being in our opinion almost certain signs of Mark's priority.

As regards the fourth reason, which was the greater intelligibility and consistency in Matthew of the presentation of the Person of Christ, to-day the very mystery and enigma of the portrait in Mark attracts us, since we think that it is likely to be nearer to the original than that in Matthew.

For indeed all the reasons thus far considered which have tended of late to reverse the traditional estimates of the relative importance of Matthew and Mark draw their cogency from the last and final contrast which we found to exist between our attitude to-day and that of the early Church. This contrast was, it will be remembered, that whereas Mark was then regarded as the epitomiser and follower of Matthew, we now have strong reason to believe that Mark is not only the earliest of the synoptic gospels, but itself also one chief source of both Matthew and Luke. And it was inevitable that this modern discovery of the temporal priority of Mark should be regarded as of immense importance, because ever since the close of the eighteenth century the subject of historical origins has been of increasing interest in all branches of study.

It should not, however, surprise us that in the early days after the discovery of the priority of Mark there was a tendency to draw from the discovery certain inferences which, unlike the

discovery itself, have not stood the test of time. At the moment
we need only consider one of these. It is this. Since St. John's
gospel is agreed to be the latest of the four, and is also obviously
the most theological gospel in the canon, the inference was
drawn that Mark, since it is the earliest, must be the least
theological of the four. It chanced also that this view blended
very well with a belief widely held at the end of the last century,
the belief that there was what we may perhaps call an original
Gospel of simple Galilean piety, of which the chief doctrines
were the Fatherhood of God and the brotherhood of man; and
that this original Gospel had become overlaid and, as some
thought, corrupted by later theological doctrine, largely owing
to the work of St. Paul. Accordingly immense pains were spent
in trying to justify and to reconstruct this early, original Gospel,
as it was believed to be, from the pages of our earliest evangelist,
St. Mark. It must be bluntly said, however, that this attempt
has proved to be a failure; it is now increasingly recognized to
have been a mistake to assume that the development in gospel-
writing was always and necessarily from the less to the more
theological; and the doctrines of the Fatherhood of God and
the brotherhood of man are not those upon which the chief
emphasis is laid in Mark. It is not always remembered that the
word 'Father' applied to God does not occur in this gospel
until the last verse of chapter 8, which is after the great dividing
line, as we may call it, of this gospel at $8^{27\,\mathrm{ff.}}$, namely, the confession by St. Peter at Caesarea Philippi.

Happily, just at the time when the study of the gospels in
this country was thus threatened by an impasse, a new method
of approach to the understanding of them, and one which
promises much more satisfactory results, was laid before us,
chiefly by Dr. C. H. Dodd of Cambridge; and for those who
may not have read his little book *The Apostolic Preaching and its
Developments*, it may be desirable to summarize his chief points,
so far as they concern us now.

He begins by asking what we can learn from the books of the
New Testament about the content of the Gospel in the earliest
days of the Church; in what form was it first proclaimed, and
what features did it include? and he proceeds to distinguish
sharply between the preaching and the teaching. The teaching,
he points out, was chiefly concerned with ethical instruction,

and although it is of course of very great importance and plays a definite though subordinate place in Mark, we need not at present dwell upon it further; but the preaching or proclaiming was concerned with new and dazzling truths about God, which were believed to have been brought to light by the coming and the work of Jesus Christ; and the author contends that we shall only understand Mark, if we regard it as designed, above all, to set forth these new Gospel-truths, on the basis of their historical origins.

Turning first to the epistles of St. Paul, as being the earliest literary sources that we have, Dr. Dodd by a survey of the evidence infers that the Gospel as preached by St. Paul certainly included at least the following elements, and may of course have included others also:

The prophecies of the Old Testament have been fulfilled, and the promised new age has been inaugurated with the coming of Jesus Christ;

Who was born of the seed of David;

Who died for us according to the scriptures, to deliver us from the power of this present evil age;

Who was buried, and rose on the third day according to the scriptures;

Who is exalted at the right hand of God, as Son of God, and Lord of quick and dead;

Who will come again as Judge and Saviour of men.

The speeches of St. Peter in the early chapters of the Acts of the Apostles are next examined, and it is found that their evidence closely agrees with that of the Pauline epistles. Thus, according to St. Peter, the age of fulfilment, that is, the messianic age, has dawned. This has taken place through the ministry, death, and resurrection of the Lord Jesus, of whose activities a brief account is given, with proof from the Old Testament scriptures that all took place 'through the determinate counsel and foreknowledge of God'. Next, in virtue of the resurrection, Jesus has been exalted at the right hand of God, as messianic Head of the new Israel; and the work of the Holy Spirit in the Church is the sign of the Lord's present power and glory. This messianic age will very shortly reach its consummation, with the manifestation of Jesus Christ in glory. Finally, therefore, men should repent, in order that they may receive forgiveness and the Holy Spirit and be saved, that is, made partakers of the life of the age to come, by entering the elect community.

On one point Dr. Dodd lays special stress:

The more we try [he says] to penetrate in imagination to the state of mind of the first Christians in the earliest days, the more are we driven to think of resurrection, exaltation, and second advent as being, in their belief, inseparable parts of a single divine event. It was not an *early* advent that they proclaimed, but an *immediate* advent. They proclaimed it not so much as a future event for which men should prepare by repentance, but rather as the impending corroboration of a present fact: the new age is already here, and because it is here, men should repent. The proof that it was here was found in the actual presence of the Spirit, that is, of the supernatural in the experience of men. It was in a supernatural world that the apostles felt themselves to be living; a world therefore in which it was natural that any day the Lord might be seen upon the clouds of heaven. That was what their Lord had meant, they thought, by saying 'The kingdom of God has come upon you', while He also bade them pray, 'Thy kingdom come'.

On this view therefore the second advent is not so much the final, supreme fact, to which all else is preparatory; rather, it is the impending verification of the Church's faith that, with the coming of Jesus Christ, heaven has descended to earth, God and man are at one; or, in more philosophical language, that the work accomplished once for all by Jesus Christ has absolute value. The purpose of the Lord's manifestation in the future is not so much to introduce a new order of things, but rather to complete that which already exists.

At first therefore, according to Dr. Dodd, the different elements in the proclamation of the Gospel formed an indivisible unity of past, present, and future; the sense of a present supernatural life, and of an overwhelming urgency, was paramount. But, as the expected immediate final vindication tarried, the unity just mentioned tended to be broken up, and a certain change of emphasis or stress became apparent, according as men dwelt upon the past or the present or the future aspect of the Lord's one work. By a brief examination of various books of the New Testament Dr. Dodd traces what he believes to have been the authentic line of development, in contrast to various degrees of over- or under-emphasis, in different quarters of the early Church. As the expectation of an immediate consummation faded, the main stream of the life of the little churches was led to concentrate attention upon the historical facts of the ministry, death, and resurrection of the Lord, framed in their messianic setting, which made clear their absolute quality as saving facts.

Let us now return to Mark, and consider whether we can gain help from the views which have just been outlined, in understanding the nature and form and contents of our earliest gospel, and also why it omits much that we should otherwise have expected to find in its pages.

We begin by examining, almost cursorily and superficially, the general outline of the book. Of the very important introduction I do not wish to speak at present. I am strongly persuaded that it consists, not, as the arrangement of the text in Westcott and Hort suggests, of the first eight verses, but of the first thirteen verses,* a point which will be found later to have considerable significance. Geographically, the remainder of the book falls into two clearly marked divisions, of almost equal length; first, the Lord's work in northern Palestine: this is described in chapters 1 to 9; and secondly, His work in and near Jerusalem; this is described in chapters 11 to 16. These two chief divisions of the book are joined together by chapter 10, which contains incidents and conversations placed between the departure from Galilee and the arrival at the capital, Jerusalem, this being the only occasion, in this gospel, on which the Lord is found at the centre of His nation's life.

We have just said that the scene of the first nine chapters is placed in Galilee, and towards their close, we may add, in the districts to the north and east of it; but it should not be overlooked that exact geographical details are almost entirely wanting. Capernaum, which is usually thought to have been a kind of headquarters of the ministry, is mentioned on three occasions; but only one of these occasions is after the first two chapters. Nazareth is not mentioned after the introduction. Bethsaida, expressly said in some words of the Lord, preserved

---

* Dr. Dodd regards the introduction as extending to verse 15 inclusive. But does not the summary of the Lord's preaching, as given in verses 14 and 15, belong more suitably to the evangelist's record of the ministry, than to his introduction?

in Matthew and Luke, to have been, along with Chorazin, the scene of several of His mighty works, is only mentioned twice; Chorazin not at all. The narrative consists for the most part of short, isolated stories, often joined to one another only by the simplest of all links, the word 'and'. Usually these stories have no precise location. The 'mountain' or hill-country, the sea-shore (meaning the strand of the Lake of Galilee), the other side of the lake, the boat, the house, a lonely place, and, in the earlier chapters, the synagogue; such is usually what we may call the stage-scenery of the Lord's ministry in Mark; and it is extremely vague.

Nor is it otherwise with notes of time. The book gives us no means whatever of judging how long the ministry lasted. At the outset the arrival of the Lord upon the scene is dated solely by a local incident, the preaching and baptism of John; 'in those days'—the days of John's activity—'Jesus cometh from Nazareth of Galilee'.* Probably the only incident from which any information on chronology can be obtained is that described in 2^{23-8}, where the disciples pluck the ears of corn, and perhaps also that in 6^{39}, where the multitude sits on the green grass. It is clearly the season of spring, and since the Lord's death also took place in the spring, we can safely postulate a ministry of at least a year, according to St. Mark; but beyond this, the book does not give us information. Clearly the interest of the evangelist and his readers did not lie in this direction.

Even a description of the Lord, as the world knew Him, is largely wanting. We are not told anything of His origin, of His development and education, of His appearance, or even of His age, although, as Wellhausen observed, it might be thought that a good deal depends upon our answer to the question whether we are to think of Him as comparatively young, or as one with a ripe experience of men and affairs. We only learn the name of His mother, and the nature of His earlier calling,†

---

* The striking contrast with Luke $3^{1\,f.}$ deserves attention. St. Luke seeks to commend the Gospel to a far wider audience than that which was envisaged by St. Mark, and he therefore dates the preaching of the Baptist by reference not only to Jewish ecclesiastical history, but to the highest secular authorities. We may compare the way in which Thucydides, at the beginning of book 2, seeks to fix the date of the Peloponnesian war.

† If we may assume that the reading followed by the Revised Version at 6^3 is correct.

because the evangelist, with a very different purpose in view, records in 6^{1-6} some derogatory remarks about Him.

The little stories themselves are told very simply and vividly. The Lord Himself is always central, either in word or in act, or in both; frequently enemies seek to oppose or provoke Him; if the disciples are present, they are seldom more than lay-figures; the crowd, of which frequent mention is made, seems to be usually the recipient of the teaching; and this teaching, though constantly mentioned, is rarely recorded by the writer. What he does repeatedly emphasize is, first, the immense impression made by the Lord, especially in consequence of His mighty acts of benevolent healing. The author almost exhausts his limited vocabulary in his descriptions of the authority and forcefulness so clearly wielded by his Master, of His power to attract and also to repel, of His quick sympathy and also, at times, of His extreme severity. We read again and again of the astonishment, bewilderment, and fear produced both by the mighty works and by the teaching. Secondly, but to a much smaller degree, the writer draws attention to the opposition which tracked the Lord's footsteps almost from the first, and to its nature, and to the classes of people who were chiefly responsible for it. Incidentally we notice that, although the stories are told very objectively, in every case of conflict the sympathy of the reader with the Lord's position is assumed.

It soon, however, becomes apparent, even on a superficial study of the book, that an analysis of it solely with reference to geography and chronology is not enough. We have already noticed that towards the end of the first half of the book, that is, towards the end of the evangelist's account of the Galilean ministry, the Lord is found chiefly outside Galilee, in the districts to the north and east of it; but this is not the only change to be noted at this point. There is now also a remarkable change in the content of the narrative, and therewith in the atmosphere. After St. Peter's acknowledgement of his Master's Messiahship at Caesarea Philippi in chapter 8, the message of the cross is set forth in no uncertain terms, both to the disciples and to the multitude. At intervals in the narrative we come upon three solemn announcements of the terrible fate in store for the Son of man; they have been strikingly compared to the solemn tolling of a minute bell, as the party makes its way from the slopes of Hermon in the far north towards Jerusalem in the south. Again, much more space is now given to the intercourse of the Lord with His disciples, as opposed to His teaching of the crowd; and the astonishment and awe excited, in the first half of the book, by His marvellous *acts*, are now connected rather with His *teaching* about the way of the cross; indeed, the mighty works themselves are all but absent from the latter half of the narrative. From time to time, however, side by side with the predictions of imminent rejection and death, we come, strangely enough, upon glimpses of glory, present or future, for the Son of man; and these shed a strange, unearthly light upon the path which the Lord is treading at the moment. Thus, almost immediately after St. Peter's confession of the Lord's Messiahship and the first proclamation of the Passion which follows hard upon it, we read of the Lord's transfiguration on a high mountain, in the presence of three disciples, in private and alone. The entrance into Jerusalem is unquestionably of a messianic character, even if there is no open proclamation. In chapter 13, more remarkably still, and once more in private, the Lord upon the Mount of Olives, using language taken from the book of Daniel, tells four disciples of the final triumph, after unspeakable horrors of good over evil, of salvation over destruction; and in one way or another it is all connected with and hangs upon the person and manifestation of the Son of man. We ought also no doubt to remember that each of the three Passion pronouncements ends with the promise of final victory through resurrection, although certainly the main purpose of the pronouncements is to assert in the strongest possible language the incredible treatment which the Son of man must undergo, before that victory is reached. We will not at this moment trench upon the evangelist's record of the message of the resurrection, but it will probably be felt to be fitting, and in conformity with all that has just been said, that the Roman centurion in charge of the crucifixion, immediately after the Lord's death, is moved to ascribe a divine sonship to Him: 'Truly this man was Son of God.'

We have occupied ourselves, in this first lecture, chiefly with two things. First, we traced the reception of this gospel in the Church. We noticed that of its immediate reception when it was first put forth and for the first fifty years and more of its circulation we know absolutely nothing, except indeed one very significant fact which I purposely did not emphasize at the moment: namely, that it was used by each of the other synoptists as a chief source. And if we are inclined to suppose that this is convincing evidence of the high regard in which the book was held, we must remember also that both St. Matthew and St. Luke undoubtedly thought that their gospels would severally supersede Mark; they would have been much surprised to find their gospels bound up together and along with Mark, to say nothing of John. We next found that, after the fourfold gospel canon was everywhere accepted, Mark has always been, till quite recently, the least noticed and the least well known of the four; and we considered the reasons for this, and also for the great change in recent times in the attention paid to it. It was suggested that the chief cause of the change was the growth amongst us of the scientific or critical spirit, leading to an interest, above all, in 'origins'.

Secondly, we glanced very cursorily at the contents of the book. We observed that geographically it falls into two clearly marked and almost equal parts; the ministry in Galilee and its neighbourhood, and the period spent in the south, chiefly in or near Jerusalem. We noticed also, however, that in addition to the two big geographical divisions of the book there is, near its centre, also a remarkable change in the atmosphere, almost, though not quite, coincident with the two geographical divisions. In the first half of the book, the interest and emphasis are on the Lord's mighty acts which are narrated in terse and vivid language; and the shadow of the cross falls only rarely, and then indirectly, on the scene.* After Caesarea Philippi, however, the mighty acts almost come to an end; and with the beginning of the journey to the south the shocking destiny in store there for the Son of man is repeatedly proclaimed; and the teaching is addressed to the disciples much more than, as has hitherto been the case, to the attendant crowd of listeners. The note of final victory indeed is repeatedly struck, but the emphasis is on the suffering, for both Master and disciples, which must precede that victory; and the long, detailed narrative of the Passion, followed by a very brief reference to the resurrection in connexion with the visit of the three women to the tomb, is in accordance

* e.g. 2^{20}, $3^{6.19}$.

with this scheme; and the book ends, as it began, with extreme abruptness; and indeed from first to last it is mysterious and baffling.

It is of course possible that, when the book was first put forth in and for some small community of Christians, very little stir was made. If, as is now widely thought, the separate stories which it embodies had been long familiar, if the Passion narrative was already a connected whole, and the doctrine of the book was already well established in the church where it appeared, then Mark may simply have been regarded as a convenient 'corpus', in book form, of the Church's accepted teaching and ·tradition. Whether this was so or not, its first readers certainly possessed one immense advantage over us; the evangelist was one of themselves, and therefore they had or could procure from the outset the key to the understanding of the book, and the knowledge how to use that key. We unfortunately are not in like case, and we are therefore likely to fumble a good deal with the lock, before the door will open to us. One great aim which I suggest that we should keep before us in these lectures is to seek to look at this gospel through the eyes of its first readers. What did the evangelist wish them to learn? What are his assumptions and his outlook? What is his purpose, and what means does he use to accomplish it? If we keep these questions steadily before us, we are more likely to refrain from putting to the evangelist questions which he was not concerned to answer, and in this way we may not only avoid any sense of disappointment with his book, but also discover what a very remarkable work, as I am persuaded, it actually is.

II

THE FIRST CHAPTER OF
ST. MARK'S GOSPEL

LET us begin by recalling Professor Dodd's reconstruction of the early preaching of the Gospel. According to him, you remember, its first item was the announcement, '*this*— that is, the recent events connected with Jesus Christ and the results of His work—*this* is that which was spoken by the prophets'; in other words, the age of fulfilment has drawn near, and the Messiah is the Lord Jesus. Next, the preaching summarized the historical facts, leading up to the resurrection of Jesus Christ and to the promise of His coming in glory; and it ended with the call to repentance and the promise of forgiveness.

We have now to consider whether and, if so, how far the plan of Mark conforms to this general scheme; and we shall do well to start with a careful examination of the introduction to the book, which we deliberately passed over previously.

If you look at Westcott and Hort's famous edition of the Greek New Testament, you will find that not only is the text most carefully divided into paragraphs, but from time to time there is, in addition to the break of a paragraph, also a space of varying size left before the new paragraph begins. In their text of Mark there are only two such breaks of the largest size; one is between verses 8 and 9 of the first chapter, and the other is at the end of the long discourse on the last things in chapter 13, before the beginning of the Passion narrative in chapter 14. At present we will concern ourselves only with the first of these, that is, the break in chapter 1. It is clear that Westcott and Hort regarded the prologue, or introduction to the gospel, as consisting of the first eight verses, and that they marked off these verses sharply from the rest of the book. These eight verses deal solely with the work of John the Baptist. By quotation from the Old Testament scriptures, and by a description of the work, appearance, and preaching of John, the evangelist shows that he regards John as the promised second Elijah, the immediate herald of the day of the Lord.

The next section, verses 9 to 13, is attached by Westcott and Hort very closely to the record of the ministry, of which accordingly, in their view, it forms a part. The Lord comes upon the scene, is baptized by John, is divinely greeted as the unique Son of God, is tempted in the wilderness, and at verse 14 comes into Galilee, where he begins to preach the Gospel.

I desire, on the contrary, to submit to you that the prologue or introduction consists, not of the first eight but of the first thirteen verses, and that the record of the ministry only begins at verse 14 with the words, 'Now after John was delivered up, Jesus came into Galilee, preaching the gospel of the kingdom of God', and so forth. This matter of the extent of the prologue is not unimportant for the understanding of the book; and I will therefore ask you to consider it more fully with me. I hope I am not unfair to those two great editors of more than sixty years ago, if I suggest that in arranging the text as they did they were unconsciously influenced by the attitude then prevalent towards the earliest gospel. For reasons which we will not now stop to consider, it was assumed that St. Mark's primary purpose was, if not to write a biography* of Jesus Christ, at any rate to set forth a plain historical narrative about Him; obviously therefore it was natural and reasonable to assume that the introduction to the book ceases, and the record proper begins, when the Lord Himself first appears upon the scene; and this happens in verse 9: 'And it came to pass in those days that Jesus came from Nazareth of Galilee.' In the last twenty-five years, however, many of us have been forced to the conclusion that this method of approach to Mark, what I may call this *primarily historical* method of approach, is an error. The matter is of course one of degree; we may confidently believe that there is much historical material of the highest value in Mark, especially as, among the four gospels, this one is nearest to the actual events; but in the last resort this evangelist's purpose is theological, rather than merely historical; or, to put the matter in another way, the historical material is being used for a theological purpose. You will remember that St.

---

* It is of interest to notice here that Dr. Salmon, in the quotation given on p. 84, calls St. Mark's gospel 'a history of our Lord'; but this is not the description of the book given in 1¹ by the evangelist himself.

Mark's opening words are, 'The beginning of the gospel of Jesus Christ, the Son of God'.* It is true that some Christian writers in the second century of our era, wishing to commend the gospels to the outside world, speak of them as 'memoirs', because they wished to give an intelligible account of the nature of the books, and the 'memoir' was a recognized type of literature at the time. But the word which St. Mark uses in his title, or headline, is not 'memoir' but 'gospel'; and the word gospel in his mouth is probably equivalent to the theme of the primitive preaching; in other words, it means 'Jesus Christ and the truth about Him'; and of this truth the historical events of His life, however important and however prominent in Mark, only form a part.

What then is the gain to us, if we believe that the introduction reaches as far as verse 13? Chiefly this, that we find placed in our hands at the outset the key which the evangelist wishes us to have, in order that we may understand the person and office of the central Figure of the book. In the first eight verses we have learned that in accordance with prophecy the second Elijah, John the Baptist, arose and prepared the way of the Lord; but we have not yet learned the identity of the greater Coming One foretold by John; only in verses 9 to 13 do we learn that He is Jesus from Nazareth of Galilee, and that He, Jesus of Nazareth, is the unique or only Son of God. By means of the story of the Lord's baptism and of the divine testimony to Him associated with it, and finally by a brief reference to the temptation, it is made clear that He, Jesus of Nazareth, is also the unspotted mirror of the Father's glory.† Satan will put forth all his energies against Him in His human nature; but He remains victorious.‡

* The Greek equivalents of the last four English words are not found in some of our authorities; but Professor C. H. Turner, one of our best guides in textual problems in Mark, sums up decisively in their favour in the *Journal of Theological Studies*, January 1927, p. 150. Professor G. D. Kilpatrick, however, tells me that the question is very difficult, and should still be regarded as open.

† According to St. Jerome the gospel according to the Hebrews recorded these words as heard by the Lord after He had ascended from the water, when 'the whole fount of the Holy Spirit descended and rested upon him': 'My son, in all the prophets I was waiting for thee that thou shouldst come and I might find rest in thee; for thou art my rest.' The words may be regarded as an excellent commentary on the canonical text.

‡ It has often been remarked that St. Mark's account of the temptation in 1¹²ᶠ· is so brief as to be barely intelligible. I am indebted to my friend Mr. H. W. Llewellyn

There is thus a close parallel, in spite of all their difference, between these thirteen verses of Mark and the first eighteen verses of John, which are usually regarded as the prologue to that gospel. Both prologues dwell upon the relation of Jesus Christ to John the Baptist, in whose appearance St. Mark and his teachers had been led to discern the return of Elijah the prophet, regarded as the immediate herald of the expected day of the Lord; and in each book it is shown that, however great and God-sent the forerunner, his work pales into insignificance when set against the arrival of Him whose way had been prepared by John. And just as St. John's prologue reaches its highest point at verse 14, 'The Word became flesh', the reference to the historic person Jesus Christ being made explicit at verse 17, 'grace and truth came by Jesus Christ', so St. Mark's prologue reaches its highest point in the words in verse 11, 'Thou art my beloved Son, in thee I am well pleased', words which are specifically addressed to Jesus, who (if we leave out of account verse 1, the headline of the book) has been first mentioned by name in verse 9, 'And it came to pass in those days that Jesus came from Nazareth of Galilee'. And finally,

Smith for the following suggestion which, if accepted, goes far to explain St. Mark's brevity here.

The contents of the synoptic gospels, especially St. Mark's, show clearly that the Lord neither regarded His Messiahship as involving a kingship of this world nor desired recognition of His Messiahship in consequence of His mighty works; and the tradition that in the course of His sojourn in the wilderness He renounced the temptation to adopt either of these courses is expressed in symbolic form in Mt. 4^{5-11} Lk. 4^{5-13}. In St. Mark's account of the temptation neither of these renunciations is expressly stated, but each is certainly implicit in his narrative. In particular the renunciation of the prompting to allow evidence of His Messiahship to be derived from His mighty acts seems to be implied in the many passages in which He is represented as deprecating publicity for His acts of power. Hence it is possible that Mk. 1^{12f}, rightly understood, forms an essential link in St. Mark's theme. In the introductory verses 1^{1-11} the Lord is made known to the reader as the Messiah. In 1^{12f} He is represented as wrestling with certain temptations. These are unspecified, but their nature is clearly supported by the whole tenor of the narrative which follows; for this makes clear that the possibility of winning recognition by the evidence of His mighty deeds had been rejected, since those recorded do not in fact lead to the recognition of Him as Messiah. St. Matthew and St. Luke, in whose gospels the injunctions to secrecy, in respect of the mighty works, are much less prominent than they are in Mark, found it desirable, when referring to the Lord's sojourn in the wilderness, to specify, by means of three symbolic scenes, the nature of the struggle which then took place. For St. Mark this was less important, since his whole treatment of the Lord's ministry seems designed to emphasize that as Messiah He renounced (*a*) a kingdom of this world, and (*b*) the working of 'signs and wonders' as a means of winning recognition.

just as in John the narrative proper only begins at verse 19, so also in Mark the narrative proper only begins with the account of the Lord's activity in verses 14 and 15, when He comes into Galilee with the announcement that the time is ripe, and God's promises are now in process of accomplishment. To quote St. Paul's words in 2 Corinthians 1[20], 'how many soever be the promises of God, in him'—that is, as St. Paul has just said in verse 19, in the Son of God, Jesus Christ—in him 'is the yes'.

Thus these introductory verses of Mark contain both a backward and a forward reference. First, with regard to the past, they recall certain beliefs of the Jews about the expected supreme intervention of their God in the events of the world's history. This intervention, which the Jews believed would bring the course of history, as it had been known hitherto, to a close, was to be prepared for, according to contemporary expectation, by the return of Elijah the prophet, who would set all things in order for the end. When therefore we read in verse 6 a description of the appearance of the Baptist, we are reminded, especially by the way in which the story is told in our present text,* of his resemblance to the prophet Elijah; and the very strong expressions in verse 5, that *all* the country of Judaea and *all* the dwellers in Jerusalem went out to him, should probably not be regarded as mere picturesque exaggeration, but emphasize what was only to be expected, at the appearance of the herald of Messiah.

And secondly, with regard to the future, the mission and work of the Baptist were essentially preparatory. His task was to warn his hearers that the anticipated divine intervention was immediately imminent, and to prepare them for it. At the time when Mark was written, that part of the Church in which this gospel arose believed that this intervention had now taken place, although it was not yet complete. In the life and work of Jesus Christ, above all in His death and resurrection, and in the life of the Church which had resulted therefrom, believers had been led to see the inauguration of the age to come. In this gospel

---

* For, if we once more follow Professor C. H. Turner, it is likely that the original reading in 1[6] was simply, 'And John was clothed with a camel's skin and ate locusts and wild honey'. If this is correct, the comparison with the appearance of Elijah (see 2 Kings 1[8]) becomes less explicit in Mark than it is in Matthew; but it need not be absent and may still explain why St. Mark draws his readers' attention to the aspect of the Baptist, although he gives no account of the aspect of the Lord.

therefore the ministry of John is presented as a prelude to and preparation for the ministry of Jesus Christ, with whose coming into Galilee the hour strikes; the era of salvation has drawn near.

I have noted, I hope rightly, that the introduction consists of the first thirteen verses of the book; but it is also clear that verses 14 and 15 are closely connected with the verses that precede them. In verses 14 and 15 the ministry in Galilee is inaugurated and a summary is given of the content of the Lord's preaching. The passage may be compared with the sermon at Nazareth, which in St. Luke's gospel forms the opening scene of the ministry. In Mark the rhythmical language emphasizes the note of solemn, triumphant rejoicing in the words, 'The time is fulfilled and the kingdom of God is at the doors;* it is your part to change your attitude of mind and to give a ready ear to the good news'. As we ponder these words, we see that they might serve equally well as a skeleton outline of the preaching of the primitive Church, with its emphasis on God's action, and men's need of repentance and faith; and indeed all our study, thus far, goes to suggest that it is the evangelist's purpose to follow the outline of the Church's proclamation of the Gospel, however much he may enlarge it by illustrations from the traditions of the life and work, and, to a less degree, the teaching of the Lord. For from this point begin the little sections, of which Mark is largely made up; and since those which follow in this chapter contain features of great interest, I will continue our examination of the first chapter in detail. Four of them seem to describe the chief events of the first sabbath of the ministry, which is spent in Capernaum, and of the morning after. But first we have verses 16 to 20, in which two pairs of brothers, Simon and Andrew, James and John, are called into the Lord's company from their trade of fishing, to become, like their new Master, fishers of men. When this gospel was written, the Christian communities were learning that they, and especially their leaders, had a peculiar responsibility as representatives of their Master. It is possible to regard the Church as the legacy of the Lord Jesus to the world. You will recall how after the words in 2 Corinthians 1²⁰ which I have already quoted—'For how many soever be the promises of God, in him'—that is, in Jesus

---

* Dr. C. H. Dodd gives the sense of the Greek here thus: 'It is the climax of all time: God's Kingdom is upon you!'

Christ,—'is the yes':—St. Paul continues—'wherefore also through him is the Amen, *to the glory of God through us*'. Thanks to the work of Jesus Christ, His followers are enabled, and it is their task, to exhibit the glory and the character of God. It is therefore fitting that St. Mark, like St. Matthew at 4$^{18-22}$ and St. John at 1$^{35-51}$ (though the latter follows a different tradition), should tell us at the outset of the story how the Lord called certain men into His company; and although in the four lists of the twelve apostles which we find in the New Testament the order of the names is different in each, yet the four men whose call is described in this little section of Mark are always placed first, and in Mark they, and particularly St. Peter, are mentioned more often than the rest.

On the sabbath day the little group enters the local synagogue, and there a signal demonstration of the Lord's power is given, both in word and in action; He teaches with authority, and He expels a demon. I am myself convinced that the second sentence of the demon's utterance is not a question, but a statement: not, 'art thou come to destroy us?', but, 'thou art come to destroy us'; and it is possible that St. Mark has assigned this very prominent position to this story, the first of its kind in this gospel, because he wishes to emphasize that one great purpose of the coming of Messiah was the destruction of the powers of evil—in the present case, spiritual evil. Probably the best commentaries on this section are, first, Mark 3^{27}: 'No one can enter into the house of the strong man'—that is, Satan, 'the prince of this world'—'and spoil his goods, except he first bind the strong man; and then he will spoil his house'; and, secondly, Ephesians 6^{1} : 'Our wrestling is not against flesh and blood'—not against human forces—'but against the principalities, against the powers, against the world-rulers of this darkness, against the spiritual hosts of wickedness in the heavenly places.' You will also notice that the teaching is not forgotten; it is expressly mentioned, along with the mighty act itself; but, as so often in this gospel, it is only alluded to in passing; its content is not actually recorded.

From public we pass to private life; in St. Peter's house his mother-in-law is restored to health. This is one of the sections in Mark, where Professor C. H. Turner invites us, and with much probability, to find direct Petrine reminiscence. He points

out that in verse 29 the reference in the word 'they' is clearly
to the Lord, Peter, Andrew, James, and John, and that therefore the form of the rest of the verse is strange. The professor
thinks that the evangelist is here rendering a personal reminiscence of St. Peter, given in the first person, into the third
person; and he suggests that if St. Peter had been accustomed
to say, 'When we had left the synagogue, we came into our
house with James and John', this would explain the form which
the sentence takes in Mark. Whether this interesting suggestion
appeals to us or not, we shall certainly do well to notice that we
have here a healing story of a very simple type, in a very precise
historical setting, to which indeed there is no exactly similar
parallel elsewhere in Mark. First, as regards the healing. The
patient is in bed with a fever; the Lord comes and raises her,
taking hold of her by the hand; the fever leaves her, and she
attends to the company's needs. There is no word of the Lord;
no note of the effect on the bystanders; simply the condition
of the patient; the act of healing; the fact of the cure, 'the fever
left her'; and finally its proof, 'she attended to their needs'.
Secondly, the precise historical setting. At the outset the party
leaves the synagogue; next, they come to Peter's house, and
their names are mentioned; and finally, although the sufferer's
name is not given, yet her identity is made clear, by the statement of her relationship to Peter. These extra details are such
as do not normally belong to the elaboration of a healing story;
they do not emphasize the cure, or bring out the meaning of the
situation, nor do they end with a chorus of praise; the narrative is
not especially striking. On the other hand, the story would lose
greatly in impressiveness, if the identity of the patient were not
mentioned. Probably therefore it was from the beginning a
story about this particular person, and historically we stand
here on firm ground.

In verses 32 to 34 we pass to the healings at sunset, and once
more the precise setting, in respect both of time and of place, is
unparalleled. It seems reasonable also to think that these three
sections must from the beginning have been closely bound together. For, immediately after the teaching and the exorcism
in the morning in the synagogue, the Lord's fame has spread
like wild-fire, as always in such cases in the East;* and at

* Professor F. C. Burkitt once drew attention to E. G. Browne's *A Year among the*

sunset, as soon as the sabbath is over and movement on any large scale becomes permissible, the door of Peter's house, to which the Lord has withdrawn, is besieged by people seeking help, and the street becomes a hospital.

To these three sections we may probably attach closely yet one more, consisting of verses 35 to 38, which describe the Lord's departure from Capernaum early next morning for prayer, and of verse 39, which forecasts an extension of His work; for it is difficult to think that these verses can at any time have stood in isolation, and the double note of time in 35, 'in the morning, a great while before day' is similar to the double note of time in 32, 'at even, when the sun did set', and perhaps helps to link the stories together.

This section, though extremely brief, contains some unusual features, to which I invite your attention. First, the associations of a 'desert place' in Mark are those of divine refreshment after strain; thus at 6³¹, when the disciples return from their evangelizing journey, the Lord says to them, 'Come ye yourselves apart into a desert place, and rest a while'. Secondly, prayer on the Lord's part is mentioned three times in this gospel: here; after the first feeding of the multitude, when He went apart into the hill-country to pray; and in Gethsemane when once more He had left the three and gone apart. The prayer, you notice, is always alone, and at night, and at times of tension. Thirdly, the expression, 'Simon and they that were with him', that is, presumably, Andrew, James, and John, is remarkable. The word 'disciples' is not used, and indeed does not occur in Mark till 2¹⁵;* possibly it would be inappropriate here, for two reasons. First, we read that they track the Lord down. The verb is only used here in the New Testament, and suggests the hunting down of an exhausted quarry. And secondly, they act not as disciples, but as interpreters of the wishes of the crowd, 'All are seeking thee'; in other words, to use a striking phrase in Dr. Nairne's *The Epistle of Priesthood*, at present they are not on the Godward but on the manward side.†

Persians, pp. 342 ff., in illustration of the results which may follow in the East when the belief spreads that a *ḥakim* is present.

 * 'Many publicans and sinners sat down with Jesus and his disciples; for there were many (sc. such disciples), and they were beginning to follow him about.'

 † There can, I think, be little doubt as to the correct interpretation of this passage; it is most unlikely that the evangelist wishes us to welcome St. Peter's

The Lord does not reply directly to the implied request in Peter's words, that, in view of the extreme interest and popularity which He has aroused at Capernaum, He should return there. Indeed it is clear that He implicitly refuses it, and in the light of the features of the story just considered, is it not probable that Capernaum has proved impossible, and He has felt bound to leave it? The two most obvious consequences of His work there on the previous day have been, first, the excitement and amazement aroused by the exorcism in the synagogue, and, secondly, the crowding of invalids in the evening at the door of Peter's house; and it is permissible to think that neither of these results was in accordance with His purpose, and that for Him the day had proved one not only of great strain but also of keen disappointment. If we are right in understanding that He left Capernaum for the sake of solitude and prayer, He now decides to continue His work elsewhere, for neither is it to be thus limited, nor is its success or failure dependent on His reception there. Should this interpretation be correct, the last words of 38, 'to this end came I forth', will refer, not, as is often supposed, to his departure from Capernaum, but to His coming forth upon His ministry in general. They will thus have been correctly interpreted by St. Luke, who in his parallel has, 'For to this purpose was I sent'.

As regards the little sections, which we have just considered, we are at liberty to think, if we wish, that they were, from the first, historically connected and represent an eye-witness's summary of the first sabbath of the ministry in Capernaum; and there is much to be said in favour of this view. If, however, we take it, we ought in justice to remember that both St. Matthew and St. Luke, by their treatment of Mark at this point, show clearly that neither of them attached any importance to this view, since they make no attempt whatever to preserve the historical connexion. As an alternative, though on the whole, for several reasons, a less probable alternative, we may suppose, if we wish, that St. Mark desires to give at the outset a picture of typical activities of Jesus Christ under the form of events

words on the ground of their testimony to the impression made by the Lord. For the verb 'to seek' is used ten times in this book, and in the other nine cases of its use it certainly has an unfavourable sense. Even if the seeking has not evil intent, as it has at 8^{11f}, 11^{18f}, 12^{12}, $14^{1.11.55}$, it is being carried out in the wrong way and is unacceptable, as at 3^{32}, 16^6. Marcan usage therefore strongly supports the interpretation of the passage which is given in the text.

loosely represented as occurring more or less within twenty-four hours; to borrow a phrase from the pastoral epistles, it is the day of the manifestation, or epiphany, of our Saviour Jesus Christ; and although God's day, that is, a sabbath, it is one of intense activity and unceasing strain for the Lord.* The typical activities presented are the call to follow, the teaching with authority, at first at any rate in the synagogue, the healing of both mind and body, the supreme impression made in word and deed, the retirement for solitude and prayer owing to the ceaseless crowding; and the constant journeying. If this is correct, it is remarkable how strongly the influence of the historic life and activities of Jesus Christ has made itself felt upon the traditional aspect of the day of the Lord, and of the coming of the kingdom of God.

The last section with which I wish to deal in this lecture is that which now follows, namely, Mark 1⁴⁰⁻⁵, the Lord's encounter with and cleansing of a leper. In strong contrast to the sections with which we have just dealt, this section seems to be entirely independent of its context on either side; so far as we can see, there is no *historical* reason why it should occur at this point in the narrative rather than at any other; and it thus serves very well to illustrate the complete independence which, as some think, was originally a characteristic of almost all the little sections of this gospel, apart from the Passion narrative. Our consideration of the passage may, however, suggest a *theological* reason for its insertion at this point.

The following points call for notice:

First, as recorded in Mark, this story has more emotional tone than any other in the four gospels, although the words descriptive of emotion—chiefly the participles employed—have almost entirely disappeared in the Matthean and Lucan parallels, and have in some cases only survived by a struggle even in our manuscripts of Mark. Thus of the leper we read, 'There cometh to him a leper, beseeching him and kneeling down to him and saying to him, If thou wilt, thou canst cleanse me'. Of the Lord we read, first, in verse 41, 'being angered'. For this is certainly more likely to be the original reading than the usual 'being

---

* We may recall the Lord's words at Jn. 5¹⁷, 'My Father is working to this very moment; I also am working', a passage which, like Mk. 1²¹⁻³⁴, itself refers to His activities on a sabbath day.

moved with compassion';* and secondly, in verse 43, 'strictly charging him'. The Greek participle here is, however, much stronger than the English rendering; the word implies indignant displeasure. We are likely to be correct in thinking that the anger and the displeasure were in no way directed against the individual leper himself, but describe the divine passionate and indignant reaction, when confronted with a signal example of the pitiful condition of hapless humanity, and all that this implied.

The second point to which I invite your attention is that the Jewish idea of uncleanness was especially associated with leprosy. No leper might approach anyone who was not similarly afflicted; the leper was regarded not only as defiled himself, but as a source of defilement to his fellows; the disease thus involved, as no other, exclusion from the community. In the New Testament the removal of other diseases is described as healing; but in all three synoptists, except for a single passage in Luke, the removal of leprosy is called cleansing. Further, the law of Moses suggested no means for the curing of leprosy. If a leper believed himself for any reason to be free from his disease, he had to submit himself for inspection by the priest, and, if certified clean, to undergo a ritual of purification and offer prescribed sacrifices. Dr. Swete, in commenting on this passage, points out that the Greek word used in the Septuagint translation of Leviticus 13 and 14 for the ceremonial purification of a leper is transferred in the gospels to the actual purging of the disease. In the light of this, may we not regard Romans 8³ as the best commentary upon the passage? 'What the law could not do, wherein it was weak through the flesh, God, sending his own Son in the likeness of sinful flesh and as an offering for sin, condemned sin in the flesh; that the ordinance of the law might be fulfilled in us, who walk not after the flesh, but after the spirit.' And St. Mark may have placed this section forthwith here, immediately after the work of the first day in Capernaum, or, if we prefer so to think, at the close of his summary account of the Lord's work in the preceding sections, for the sake of the strong light which it throws upon the surpassing nature of the salvation now accessible to men.

* Professor C. H. Turner (*J.T.S.*, January 1927, p. 157) gives the reasons which 'dictate decision' here.

I will end this lecture by some further remarks upon the little sections which are so conspicuous a feature of this gospel. It is widely believed at the present time, as I have already said, that the stories contained in the little sections were handed down in the early Church, whether orally or in writing or in both ways together, at first as separate, independent units; and that when they came to be linked together, as we have them now, whether this task was first accomplished by St. Mark or, as is more probable, to some extent by his predecessors in evangelic writings, they were often grouped according to similarity of theme or content rather than for reasons of chronological order. No doubt the position of some of the stories is decided by the nature of their contents. Thus the call of disciples is likely to be near the beginning of the ministry, and the events which led directly to the crucifixion must be near its close. But St. Mark seems to have been free to use his own discretion as regards the setting of many of the stories; and tradition itself states that his gospel did not set down in order the things that were either done or said by the Lord. This was indeed almost inevitable if the stories at first, as is probable, simply passed independently from mouth to mouth; it is uncertain how soon they were first written down, and whether this was done long before St. Mark took up his pen or whether he was the first or almost the first to do it.

We may notice here two interesting points in the use of Mark made by the two later synoptic writers, St. Matthew and St. Luke. These evangelists after all are by a very long way our earliest authorities on Mark; we might almost call them, in certain respects, the earliest commentators known to us on his book; and it is therefore important to watch them in their use of it. The two points which I wish now to emphasize are these. First, they attach very little weight to the order of the stories as given in Mark. We have already had an example of this before us above. It is especially true of St. Matthew, who, if he was aware of the frequently subtle and delicate arrangement by St. Mark of his material, seems to have been strangely ready to destroy it, presumably owing to the importance which he attached to certain other interests. If therefore we are inclined to search for chronological arrangement in Mark and to attach importance, for this reason, to the order of its sections, we ought in fairness to remember that the two authorities known to us, who first used the book, and, we may add, comparatively soon after its publication, did not find its value in the chronological order of the little sections.

And secondly, the majority of the stories in Mark contain as their chief and usually central feature a notable saying of the Lord; and it is worthy of notice that St. Matthew and St. Luke, although in their use of Mark they are apt to treat the introductions and conclusions of the sections with considerable freedom, usually follow Mark closely in this central feature. In the outward wrappings of the stories there is thus a large measure of diversity; but the central core or kernel is usually preserved and recorded with little alteration.

The next matter to which I wish to refer in connexion with the sections, is the second-century tradition that St. Mark's gospel is based on the evangelist's remembrance of St. Peter's information. I hope that this may well be so, as regards certain sections and details of this gospel; but the tradition can hardly be pressed, to the extent either of claiming a connexion of St. Peter with the contents of the book as a whole, or of asserting that the stories have come down to us exactly as he told them. It is difficult to express at once briefly and cogently the reasons for this judgement. At the moment it must suffice to say this: the way in which most of the stories are told does not suggest that they give us, almost at first hand, an eyewitness's account of the doings of the Lord. The form in which these lie before us in Mark implies rather that they are likely to have circulated for some time in the tradition of the Church, and that this process has left its mark upon them. In course of time *this* point has been emphasized and *that* neglected, in accordance with the prevailing interests of those who told and heard the stories. Many of the difficulties which perplex us as we study the book may be due to this cause. I could have illustrated this point at length when we considered St. Mark's story of the cleansing of a leper by the Lord.

The last observation which I wish to make at this stage with reference to the little sections of Mark is this. If it be true that the book is an expanded form of the original preaching of the saving events which formed the foundation of the Gospel, it becomes of great importance and interest to inquire, with regard

to each of the little sections which the evangelist has incorpor-
ated, What has this section to teach us, not only of historical
truth, but of the saving power of the Gospel? Why was the
memory of this particular story preserved and cherished in
the early Church? What Gospel-truth does it enshrine? For the
sake of an illustration, let me refer here to the group of five
stories in Mark, which follow immediately on the sections
which we have considered to-day; four in chapter 2, and one
at the beginning of chapter 3: namely, the stories of the healing
of the palsied man; of the call of Levi followed by the banquet;
of the question about fasting, in connexion with the disciples of
John; of the plucking of the ears of corn by the disciples on the
sabbath day; and of the healing of the man with the shrunken
hand, or arm. Since in all these five stories the Lord is found in
conflict with opponents, they are often called conflict-stories;
and such indeed they are. But they are also, and much more,
Gospel-stories; for each contains some great saying of the Lord,
which has a vital bearing on the content of the Gospel-message.
Let me read the five sayings in order, one from each of the five
stories; and consider, if you will, how valuable they are, in
connexion with the Christian Gospel:

The son of man has authority to forgive sins on the earth.
I came not to invite righteous men, but sinners.
Can the sons of the bridechamber (that is, the friends who are most
closely connected with the bridegroom, can they) mourn, while the
bridegroom is with them?
The Son of man is lord even of the sabbath.
Is it lawful on the sabbath day to do good? or is it lawful to do evil?
is it lawful on the sabbath day to save a life? or is it lawful to destroy it?

As regards this last saying, its Gospel-connexion will become
clear, when we recall that the speaker will at the very next
moment reveal Himself as a *Saviour* of life, by restoring a shrunk-
en limb to full efficiency.

We are now half-way through these lectures, and yet we
have only been able to deal with a very small fraction of this
gospel. But it is, I hope, already clear in what way I desire to
suggest that we as students shall best approach the study of it.
We should remember always that we are dealing with a gospel,
and that a gospel is not the same thing as a history. The little

stories, which for the most part make up St. Mark's volume, record events which were believed, on the testimony of eye-witnesses or of the general tradition, to have taken place some thirty or forty years earlier. But they were not written down only or chiefly because they were of great historical interest, and nothing more. The stories were told because of their permanent value, as saving truth, to the successive readers of the book, and it was no doubt assumed that these readers would verify for themselves, to a very large extent, the saving truths illustrated by the stories. Hence, on one side the stories deal with events which took place, once for all, in Palestine; and as historical students we seek and rightly seek to ascertain how far they are reliable as historical narratives and here we are and must be, no doubt, to a large extent in the hands of the experts. But there is another side, with regard to which we may find out how far they are reliable, and on which we are our own masters; and this side is of even more importance, since the question is now of the religious life itself. On this side students of the gospels have not finished with the stories until their immediate religious relevance is seen; what they teach about the permanent relationship of God and man; and, above all, what response accordingly is made to them.

III

THE LORD'S MESSIAHSHIP IN
ST. MARK'S GOSPEL

IT is well known that we have very little information about
the life and death of Jesus Christ from any other than Christian
sources; the references to Him in pagan or in non-Christian
Jewish literature are extremely few. Dr. T. W. Manson, however, in an interesting paper published in the John Rylands
Library Bulletin, March 1944, emphasizes that all our sources,
pagan, Jewish, and Christian alike, at least agree in one point,
namely, that He was a crucified teacher. The *differentia* of the
Christian statement, that which distinguishes it sharply from
the other two sources, is the additional assertion that this crucified teacher is the Messiah of Jewish expectation, and indeed
much more than the Jewish Messiah. This core of the Christian
message, that the crucified one is also Messiah and Lord of all,
is conspicuous in St. Paul's epistles: 1 Corinthians 1²³, 'we
proclaim a Messiah crucified, to Jews a stumbling block, and
to Gentiles foolishness'; 1 Corinthians 2², 'I determined not to
know anything among you, except Jesus Christ, and him
crucified'; and Galatians 3¹, 'O foolish Galatians, . . . before
whose eyes Jesus Christ was set forth, placarded, as crucified';*
and we may say, subject to certain reservations to be considered
in this lecture, that the crucified Messiah, as the fulfilment of
God's promise to His people, is also the chief theme of St. Mark's
gospel. Of the Lord's teaching St. Mark gives us very little; for
that, we have to turn above all to the non-Marcan material
common to Matthew and Luke; and when St. Mark does record
teaching at any length, he does so, as I hope we shall see, not so
much because of its surpassing value, as for a particular reason
connected with the general purpose of his book. But he does
dwell at great length, directly and more often indirectly, upon
the Lord's Messiahship and its nature; and it is to this subject
that I now wish to draw your attention.

I have already pointed out that the *reader* of this gospel is

---

* The suggestion has been made that the Greek word used by St. Paul here may
refer to the recitation, in the worship of the Church, of the events of the Passion.

admitted to a knowledge of the Lord's Messiahship in the introduction. Probably one great purpose of the book is to instruct or to remind the reader, as the story advances, of the surprising and surpassing nature and quality of that Messiahship, as interpreted, on Christian principles, in the light of the cross; but the *fact* of the Lord's office and function is expressly put before the reader at the outset. The title of the book, as we have it, is 'The beginning of the Gospel of Jesus Christ, Son of God'; and in the prologue, at the Lord's first appearance on the scene, He is forthwith greeted with the divine salutation, 'Thou art my beloved' (or rather, only*) 'Son; in thee I find full pleasure'. The words imply the perfection, divinity, and sinlessness of Him to whom they are addressed. Part, therefore, of the purpose of the introduction to this gospel is to place the reader, *unlike those who first actually came in contact with the Lord*, in possession of the fact of His Messiahship.

But I ought not to omit to refer to another way of approach to the story of the Lord's baptism in Mark, and to explain why it does not seem to me entirely satisfactory.

It is often said that St. Mark records the divine witness given to the Lord at His baptism, in order to show how the latter became aware of His office, function, and vocation. On this view the narrative is similar to those of the Old Testament in which we read of prophets being called and commissioned for their office; and the scene is recorded in Mark, primarily because it deals with a crisis in the Lord's life and was of surpassing importance to Him; while the narrative of the threefold temptation which follows in Matthew and Luke shows Him reflecting upon the way in which He is to use the powers of the office which He now knows to be His.

St. Mark's record gives us every reason to believe that the time of the baptism and the withdrawal which followed it were probably a critical period in the Lord's experience, and it is natural that speculation should wish to consider reverently what the significance of this period may have been to Him; but we should, I suggest, be mistaken in thinking that the interpretation above gives us the chief or primary reason for St. Mark's procedure here. I beg you to recall once more the reasons

---

* For a convincing justification of the translation 'only' or 'unique', rather than 'beloved', see Professor C. H. Turner's article in *J.T.S.*, Jan. 1926.

which I put forward for regarding the story of the Lord's baptism as forming part of the prologue to the gospel, not of the record of the ministry; and a prologue is especially designed to make clear to the reader how he is to understand the contents of the book which follow the prologue. If we were right in comparing Mark 1$^{1-13}$ in certain respects with John 1$^{1-18}$, the prologue to the fourth gospel, then Mark 1$^{10f.}$, where we read of the Lord seeing the heavens rent asunder and hearing the voice of His divine acceptance, is St. Mark's equivalent or counterpart to John 1^{14}, 'the Word became flesh'; and our earliest evangelist's chief purpose in making use of the divine testimonies which are said to have accompanied the baptism is in order to proclaim the incarnation. On this view they are much more than a revelation of the Lord's mind at a particular moment.

Similarly, although I now speak with greater hesitation, I think it is open to question whether the scene near Caesarea Philippi is meant to describe the *first* acknowledgement by the disciples of their Master's Messiahship; that it is in fact a divinely granted discovery by St. Peter, made by him for the first time at this moment. The belief that the words are such a discovery is widespread; thus Professor Burkitt calls it a momentous occasion and says that Peter and the disciples are now put for the first time on the same footing as the demons, who alone up to this point in Mark have confessed the divine office and function of the Lord. I am not quite convinced that St. Mark meant his readers to understand the passage in this way. I think that here too we may be ascribing to his record the interpretation of it which we find most congenial to the strong psychological interests of the present time. The evangelist, however, may have been thinking not so much of the contrast between a previously unenlightened and now suddenly enlightened Peter, as of the contrast between those who perceive and confess the divine nature and office of the Lord, however and whenever they may have gained this knowledge, and those who in St. Paul's words still only know Him after the flesh. For the Lord has just asked His disciples, as they walk together, 'Who do *men* say that I am?' that is, what does the *world* say about me? and he has received answers which show that popular opinion ascribes to Him high roles indeed—John the Baptist, Elijah, one of the prophets—but all of them roles of preparation, not the one final role of fulfilment, consummation, of the *achievement* of salvation. The question is then renewed to *them*: But *you*, you who form the nucleus of the new Israel, you, to whom has been given the mystery of the kingdom of God, you, whom I have called and chosen, who have consorted with me, who do *you* say that I am? And I suggest that St. Peter's reply, 'Thou art the Messiah', should perhaps be taken rather as his and his fellow disciples' acknowledgement and confession of their Master's person and office, owing to their inner *knowledge* of Him, in contrast to the *opinion* of the world about Him, than as a first and unrelated discovery, at that moment, by St. Peter. And if it should be urged that the encomium pronounced upon St. Peter at this point in Matthew is most easily understood, if this occasion was indeed the first acknowledgement of the Lord's Messiahship, I should reply that in many contexts St. Matthew by no means shows a perfect understanding of his chief authority Mark, and if indeed he did think that this was the first such occasion, is inconsistent with himself.*

It will thus be evident that I am distrustful of attempts to find in this gospel a record either of the mental and spiritual development of the Lord or of the steps by which His disciples were led to a knowledge of His person. I doubt whether it was part of the evangelist's purpose to show either how the Lord Himself came to a knowledge of His office and destiny or how the faith of the disciples in Him deepened and developed. We need always to remember that interest in such matters is of very modern growth, and I believe that we do St. Mark an injustice in thinking that he and his first readers regarded these matters as we do. A careful study of the gospel itself suggests that it is indeed designed to answer certain questions and to meet certain difficulties, though not those which naturally occur to *us*; and perhaps we are likely to be least wide of the mark if we think of the evangelist as seeking, by means of some of the available traditions, to build up his readers' faith by answering these questions and meeting these difficulties. Let us consider what some of them are likely to have been.

---

* For we read at Matt. 14³³, *before* the events near Caesarea Philippi, that when the Lord rejoined His disciples in the boat on the lake they 'worshipped him, saying, Of a truth thou art the Son of God'. A comparison with the Marcan parallel, Mark 6⁵¹ᶠ·, is instructive here.

We are working on the assumption, which is at least as probable as any other, that this gospel was written in and destined for the church at Rome. This church from the first included, as we know from St. Paul's epistle to the Romans, both Jews and Gentiles. Among St. Mark's purposes in writing his gospel would certainly be the confirmation of both these classes of people in their grasp and understanding of the faith, although I am inclined to think that he envisages a Gentile even more than a Jewish audience. We know from 1 Corinthians 1[23] that both Jews and Gentiles were offended by the doctrine of a crucified Messiah. To the Jews such a doctrine was a stumbling-block, because a crucified Messiah was the precise opposite of Jewish convictions and hopes. The Jewish Messiah was to be the glorious vindicator of Israel and Israelite ideals against the wicked cruelty and godlessness of the world empires. But crucifixion was a Roman punishment; and therefore a crucified Messiah was a Messiah delivered over to and defeated by that mightiest and, to many Jews of the first century A.D., most hateful of all the empires of the world. A crucified Messiah was a contradiction in terms.

Again, to the Gentiles a crucified Messiah was foolishness, because to them the word Messiah implied a Jewish national leader, and therefore a crucified Messiah meant a dangerous agitator very properly put out of the way by the imperial authorities. A justly convicted criminal of this kind could not conceivably be regarded as a potential 'saviour' or 'benefactor' of mankind, such as the Gentile world could welcome.

A crucified Messiah was thus the supreme paradox of Christian faith; and even in the first half of the book this thought is never long absent from the mind of the evangelist. It is, however, at first hidden from all those who come in contact with the Lord, and, before we go further, some remarkable features of the book in this connexion should be noticed.

First, for reasons which can perhaps without difficulty be guessed if we consider what the word Messiah had previously been thought to imply, the evangelist seldom applies the actual title Messiah to the Lord. The word Christ, which is the Greek equivalent of the Hebrew word Messiah, only occurs in the best texts of Mark seven times. Thus in 1[1] the words Jesus Christ are almost certainly a proper name; in 8[29] the word is used in

St. Peter's confession; in 9⁴¹ the disciples are said to belong to Christ; in 12³⁵, 13²¹ the word is used of the expected Jewish Messiah, without direct reference to the Lord Himself; and in 14⁶¹, 15³², at the close of the book it is applied to Him by opponents. In order to express the Lord's nature, function, and office St. Mark seems to prefer other terms, such as Son of God, Only Son, Holy One of God, Son of man; and it is therefore important to remember, if we are to regard this lecture as a consideration of St. Mark's treatment of the nature of the Lord's Messiahship, that we are using the term as representative of all the terms found in the book to describe the divine person of the Lord.

And secondly, even if the chief theme of this gospel may be rightly described as that of the crucified Messiah, it should be noticed that not only the Lord's Messiahship but also the fact of His coming crucifixion are not represented in Mark as being apparent throughout to those, whether disciples or opponents, who consorted with Him; the latter, like the former, is only revealed to all men at the crisis of the story. Neither the substantive cross nor the verb to crucify occurs in Mark, except the noun used metaphorically in the phrase 'to take up the cross' at 8³⁴, until chapter 15, which describes the actual crucifixion; in it the words occur ten times. In the last half of the book, in the three proclamations to the disciples about the coming Passion and also elsewhere, the Lord has made it clear that He must die, and in the third proclamation it has been stated that He will be handed over to the Gentiles; but just as in the first half of the book the Messiahship is unknown to all and in the second half known only to disciples, until the actual acknowledgement of it by the Lord Himself when He stands before the Jewish tribunal which condemns Him, so the precise nature of His death is only revealed in the course of the scene which immediately precedes it. It behoves us therefore to bear these qualifications carefully in mind, if none the less we venture to say that the chief theme of St. Mark's gospel is that of the crucified Messiah. The full nature of the tragedy and of its paradox is only very gradually revealed.

The first half of the book is largely occupied with descriptions of the Lord's mighty works or acts of power. There are twelve of these in all in Mark, and ten of them occur before St. Peter's confession at Caesarea Philippi; in other words an overwhelming proportion of them is found in the first half of the book. We may say with some confidence that to St. Mark and his readers these mighty acts of benevolence are certainly evidences of the Lord's Messiahship; but the evangelist is careful to make clear that they were not thus regarded at the time when they were actually performed. They were received, it is true, with overwhelming amazement and awe, but they do not lead to a confession of Messiahship, at any rate by the majority of those who witnessed them; and when the demons, who are regarded as possessing spiritual insight, acknowledge the presence of their conqueror, silence is enjoined upon them. Even on the two occasions in the first half of the book when the mysterious expression 'the Son of man' is used, no notice is taken or comment passed by those who hear it. Part of St. Mark's purpose may be to emphasize that the Lord's conduct, in spite of the great impression which He made, was wholly free from any effort to arouse public excitement, which indeed He did His utmost to suppress; and that it gave no colour whatever to a charge of seditious messianic activity.* The Lord is not represented in these chapters as drawing attention to His person, but from time to time the evangelist shows his readers that there is a secret about Him and His work. The events which are taking place are concerned with something which is not apparent on the surface. In one context 4¹¹ this is called the mystery of the kingdom of God† and is said to have been granted to the disciples, in spite, we may add, of the lack of perception and insight for which they are frequently rebuked in Mark. One considerable part then of the first eight chapters is devoted to the mighty works of the Messiah, although at the time these were not recognized as such.

Another principal theme which occupies a great part of these early chapters and indeed also (unlike the mighty works) a

---

* Here and elsewhere in this lecture I am much indebted to J. H. Ropes's *The Synoptic Gospels*, Harvard University Press, 1934, a book which, unless I am mistaken, is too little known in this country.

† It is sometimes said that in the first half of the book the Lord proclaims the kingdom of God; but the statistics hardly allow us to take this view. The expression occurs fourteen times in Mark, and seven of these occasions, as it happens, are in chaps. 9 and 10. In the first half of the book the term is only used, apart from 1¹⁵, three times in chap. 4 and at 9¹.

great part of this gospel throughout, is the opposition which the Lord encountered, and the unworthy causes of it.

I have already drawn attention to the group of conflict-stories in 2^1 to 3^6, the last of which ends with a resolve, on the part of the Lord's opponents, to destroy Him. If it be said that such a resolve on their part at this very early stage is difficult to credit, the reply may be offered that the evangelist, who is using these little stories partly in order to explain the origins and causes of the hostility encountered by the Lord, wishes in this concluding note to remind the reader of the issue which the conflicts had, namely, the Lord's death through the machinations of the leaders of His people. As I have said, we notice elsewhere in these stories that the shadow of the end begins to fall across the scene; we may recall especially 2^{20}, 'The days will come, when the bridegroom shall be taken away from them'. Towards the end of chapter 3, the opposition takes a darker turn. For the first time we hear of scribes coming from *Jerusalem*, who attribute the Lord's healing powers to satanic origin, and draw from Him the crushing reply that Satan can hardly be fighting against Satan. Chapter 6 contains two passages, which carry on the sombre theme of opposition. First, the Lord is rejected in his own home-country, a rejection which, as treated by St. Luke, is certainly represented as a symbol, or illustration, *in petto*, of the Lord's rejection by His nation at large; and it is probable that in Mark also this thought is in the mind of the evangelist. And secondly, the story of the execution of John the Baptist by the petty tyrant Herod Antipas is told at length. We scarcely need to learn from a remark of the Lord later in this gospel* that in the death of the forerunner is to be seen clearly enough a picture of the fate reserved for Himself.

Two more conflicts with Pharisees are recorded before we come to Caesarea Philippi. In these, the Lord seems to take an almost aggressive attitude towards them. In chapter 7 they are severely attacked for their excessive devotion to tradition; in this section only in Mark do we find the word 'hypocrites' in a saying of the Lord; and in chapter 8 when they ask for a sign from heaven, the refusal is extremely abrupt; and in the original it contains two very strong asseverations in the

* 9^{13}.

words, 'Amen, I say to you, no sign shall be given to this generation'.*

Thus two principal constituent elements of the first half of this gospel are, on the one hand, the Lord's mighty works, and, on the other, the unceasing hostility of the religious and political leaders. There remain, however, two other passages, not yet considered, which though subsidiary are of considerable importance.

In the first place, we read that steps are taken to meet the menace of the increasing opposition. In chapter 3, after the last conflict-story, the Lord in this gospel finally leaves the synagogue (if we neglect the single occasion in chapter 6, to which I alluded just now, when He teaches in the synagogue 'in his own country' on the sabbath day). After withdrawing from the synagogue in chapter 3, He first meets a great multitude of enthusiastic followers on the shore of the lake, and proceeds to make a selection from them, with whom He withdraws to the high ground; and we then read of the appointment of the twelve, and a list is given of their names. We may see here, if we choose, the foundation of the new Israel, Israel after the flesh having proved itself unworthy; in any case the scene as a whole, 3^{7-19}, is certainly a beacon light in the midst of the darkness on either side of it.

Very much the same purpose is traceable in chapter 4, the so-called 'parables chapter'. It will be remembered that the first thirty-four verses of this chapter, consisting almost entirely of the Lord's teaching which includes three parables, form a remarkable exception to the usual procedure of the evangelist, who constantly refers to the Lord's teaching but very seldom gives examples of it. Indeed, the only close parallel to 4^{1-34} in Mark is the long discourse on the last things in chapter 13; and the evangelist's motive is probably in each case the same. For the present let us confine ourselves to chapter 4.

It was suggested, earlier in this lecture, that one principal theme of this gospel is 'Messiah crucified', and that even in the first half of the book this thought is never very far away. In chapters 2^1 to 3^6 St. Mark has been giving examples of the

* For it combines the solemn New Testament phrase 'Amen, I say to you' with the semitic form of vehement negation, often so translated in the LXX. '[May I perish,] if a sign shall be given to this generation.'

hostility offered to the Lord, that hostility which ended in the cross. But if it is God's Messiah who is thus opposed and rejected, then this opposition and rejection are not final; the purpose of God can be discerned in them; and the last word must be victory, not defeat. St. Paul, after saying in I Corinthians I that Christ crucified is to Jews a stumbling-block and to Gentiles foolishness, continues, 'but to them that are called, both Jews and Greeks, Christ the power of God and the wisdom of God'; and this thought can be applied to chapter 4 of Mark. Thus the parables and the sayings which accompany them are not narrated at this point in order to give typical examples of the Lord's methods in teaching; they have a particular and identical purpose. They seem to be intended to give the Lord's own explanation of the meaning of His ministry. Varied as the parables and sayings are, they all strike one note: ultimate success in spite of manifold hindrance. When seed is sown in a field, very much is certain to be lost; but, equally, much will fall on good ground and will produce a harvest, and a great one, some of it of the highest quality. Again, a lamp is intended and destined to give forth its light, not to be obscured and useless. If treasure has to be hidden for a time, it is only in order that it may some day be produced; it does not remain concealed for ever. Again, we all know that a farmer has labours and troubles in plenty; he must plough, harrow, and weed; and no doubt many dangers—bad weather, insects, disease—all threaten the seed; but if he is wise, he will not be consumed with daily anxiety about the growth of his crop; the earth of its own accord—or, if we prefer it, God—will give the silent, mysterious, all-important increase, ending or culminating in the harvest. And finally a mustard seed, if the principle of life is in it, even though it be so small that we can hardly see it, will in due course produce a great bush.

The same note runs throughout; final success in spite of temporary hindrance; if a work or purpose be of God it cannot be defeated; rather, the temporary hindrance has its part to play. In the language of the last half of this gospel, if the son is put to death, that is not defeat, nor is it the end. It is true that owing to our ignorance of the original occasion and context of many sayings of the Lord it is sometimes difficult to say with confidence what their immediate meaning and purpose will have been; but at any rate the motive of the evangelist in bringing these parables and sayings together at this point is tolerably clear.

We now reach the very significant events connected with the neighbourhood of Caesarea Philippi. It is noticeable that when St. Peter answers the Lord's question with the words 'Thou art the Christ', the title is neither accepted nor refused; but, for it, is substituted at once another title, the Son of man; and this august title is forthwith associated with rejection, suffering, death, and resurrection; and it is this combined theme which dominates the rest of this gospel. We read that by divine necessity a very terrible lot is in store for the Son of man; but at the same time very great stress is silently laid on the significance of the term thus used.

It is well known that many difficulties are connected with the interpretation of the semitic term 'the Son of man' which is frequently used by the Lord, and by Him only, in the gospels. On the one hand, it certainly emphasizes a connexion with humanity. We may recall Psalm 8[4],

> What is man, that thou art mindful of him?
> And the son of man, that thou visitest him?

where the Hebrew poetic parallelism shows that the term here is the equivalent of 'man'. On the other hand, its significance in the New Testament is almost certainly connected with its use in Daniel 7[13], 'There came with the clouds of heaven one like unto a son of man', where it is made clear, later in the same chapter, that the reference is to 'the saints of the Most High', implying the 'elect' or 'remnant' of Israel.

Certain points may be briefly mentioned, on which there is a large measure of agreement about the meaning of the term in pre-Christian Judaism. First, it includes the conception of an ideal or supernatural Power, and the establishment of a divine kingdom upon earth is committed to this Power. Secondly, in spite of the term's apparent emphasis on humanity, its technical Jewish use had resulted in an equal emphasis on the connexion of the Son of man with God, as against the nations of the world; and therefore it tended to suggest a fundamental contrast between God and the world, and, above all, between God and sinners. In the light of this, such passages as Mark 2[1-12] and 14[41] gain greatly in significance. A third point may be put forward in the words of Dr. T. W. Manson, who thinks that the expression is in the gospels 'the final term in a series of conceptions, all of which are found in the Old Testament'. These are: the Remnant (Isaiah), the Servant of Jehovah (2 Isaiah), the 'I' of the Psalms, and the Son of Man (Daniel). He proceeds to ask how it comes about that in the gospels the term is often and obviously a designation of the Lord Himself. It is, he says, because, as an outcome of the Lord's prophetic ministry, the application of the term became restricted to Him only.

His mission is to create the Son of Man, the Kingdom of the saints of the Most High, to realize in Israel the ideal contained in the term. This task is attempted in two ways: first by public appeal to the people through the medium of parable and sermon and by the mission of the disciples: then, when this appeal produced no adequate response, by the consolidation of his own band of followers. Finally, when it becomes apparent that not even the disciples are ready to rise to the demands of the ideal, he stands alone, embodying in his own person the perfect human response to the regal claims of God.*

This quotation may be supplemented and completed by the last words of an essay by Sir Edwyn Hoskyns on 'Jesus the Messiah': 'in the end the particularity of the Old Testament is only intelligible in the light of its narrowed fulfilment in Jesus, the Messiah, and of its expanded fulfilment in the Church'.†

In any case the distinctive feature in the New Testament use of the term is the combination of the term 'the Son of man' with necessary suffering and death; and nowhere is this combination more strongly emphasized than in the last half of this gospel. Between 8[27] and 16[8] the term occurs in twelve contexts, in nine of which it is connected with service, suffering, and death, and only in three with a future coming in power and glory. So far as we know, there had previously been little, some would say no, blending of the figure of the suffering Servant in Isaiah 40 to 55 with that of the Messiah; and the evangelist interweaves with great skill these two aspects of his theme, the suffering and the glory. The collocation of the Transfiguration with the first proclamation of the Passion and, as we may call it, the way of the cross, is a good example of this combination. For it is not

* *The Teaching of Jesus*, p. 227 f.
† *Mysterium Christi*, p. 89.

likely to be accidental that within a week after the disciples
have heard the first proclamation of the Passion, a precise note
of time which is otherwise unparalleled in St. Mark's record of
the ministry, three of their leaders are taken by their Master
into the hill-country in private and alone, that they may for a
moment behold Him in the fullness of His supernatural Being.

There is a tendency in some quarters at the present time to
regard the Transfiguration, which is thus placed by St. Mark
at the centre of his gospel, as having been originally an appearance of the Lord after the resurrection. Although those who
hold this view can appeal to the great name of Wellhausen in
support of it, some good reasons can be given why we should be
cautious in adopting it. In the first place, all accounts in the
gospels of appearances of the risen Lord begin in His *absence*.
After His arrival He *speaks*, and His words are an essential
element in the process of making Himself known to His hearer
or hearers; sometimes also He *acts*; whereas at the Transfiguration He is present from the beginning, and silent throughout.
Again, from the story of the draught of fishes in John 21, and
its sequel in the restoration of St. Peter, we know what is the
content of a Resurrection appearance in which St. Peter was
concerned; and this story in John 21, in view of the recent
denial of the Lord by St. Peter, naturally has indirect reference
to that denial, in the fact of his threefold restoration and commission. But in the story of the Transfiguration, St. Peter is
simply one along with St. James and St. John; he is in no way
singled out, either for rebuke or restoration. And thirdly, why
should Moses and Elijah appear in a vision of the *risen* Lord?
In the Transfiguration story, however, as recorded in Mark,
their presence may be regarded as of great significance. They
are regarded as inhabitants of the realm of light, into which the
Lord is momentarily transformed, and they converse with Him.
St. Peter in his halting, frightened utterances equates the three
celestial figures, Moses, Elijah, and the Lord. 'Let us make three
tabernacles [or tents], one for thee, and one for Moses, and one for
Elijah'. (In Jewish language, 'to dwell in a tent' is a recognized
phrase for the mode of dwelling by a divine being among men.)
But the heavenly voice corrects his error; 'this (person only), *he*
is my unique *Son*; hear ye *him*'. Henceforth the Lord alone is to
claim their allegiance; Moses and Elijah, the representatives in

the old dispensation of law and prophecy respectively, yield place to Him who as the author of the new dispensation now fulfils them both. In the language of Luke 16[16], 'The law and the prophets were until John; from that time the gospel of the kingdom of God is proclaimed'. In the heavenly voice at the Transfiguration we have a clear parallel to Mark 1[11], 'Thou art my unique [or only] Son, in thee I find full pleasure'; but whereas there the voice is directed only to the Lord Himself, here it is addressed to the three persons whom the Lord had taken apart. Indeed, if we read St. Mark's version of the Transfiguration carefully, without thought of the parallel versions in Matthew and Luke, we find that in Mark the whole event, from first to last, takes place solely for the sake of the three disciples. 'He was transfigured *before them*'; 'there appeared *unto them* Elijah with Moses'; 'there came a cloud overshadowing *them*'; 'this is my only Son; hear *ye* him'; 'and suddenly, looking round about, they saw no one any more, save Jesus only *with themselves*'. For the reader, as originally for the three disciples themselves, the story of the Transfiguration sets the seal of the divine approval on the teaching, just given, about the way of the cross, and attests also the divine nature of the Person giving it.

At an earlier stage in these lectures I drew your attention to the great change in the atmosphere of the narrative after Caesarea Philippi. The stories of mighty works almost cease; the teaching becomes more prominent, but is now imparted chiefly to professed disciples, while the crowd tends to fall into the background; and awe, religious fear, and amazement are henceforth evoked, not as before by the mighty works, but by the nature of the teaching given, and sometimes by the mere fact of the presence of the Lord.

The last half of chapter 9 is introduced by the second proclamation of the Passion,* and this is followed by renewed instruction on the inseparable connexion of suffering and discipline, inevitable both for the Master Himself and for the twelve who follow Him, with the work and the cause of the Son of man. Thus to dispute who is the greatest betrays gross misunderstanding; and to reject any friends, however incoherent

---

* Attention may be called to the brevity of this second proclamation (remarkable in all the synoptic gospels, especially Luke) and to the fact that in Mark the first verb is in the present tense.

or imperfect their allegiance, can only be regarded as a sign of arrogance. In chapter 10 we have the journey southwards towards the capital, and in the middle of the chapter we find the last and most precise prediction of the coming Passion. We should notice that this last prediction contains for the first time the warning that the Son of man will be handed over, by the leaders of the Jewish nation, to the *Gentiles*; the implications of this most important fact do not become apparent until we reach the Passion narrative itself, and had better not be considered till we come to it. On either side of this last prediction of the Passion are sections designed to illustrate or emphasize the truths about the necessity of sacrifice and service already laid down in the preceding chapter.

In chapter 11 the Lord enters Jerusalem, riding, as Zechariah had prophesied, on the beast of peace.* The passage is not free from difficulty, but certainly the evangelist wishes his readers to discern in the acclamations of the pilgrims the welcome, it may have been on the part of some an unconscious welcome,† given to the Messiah on His arrival at the capital, and also in His own action in sending for the colt His acceptance of the office. Almost immediately, however, the clash between Him and the representatives of what we may now begin to call the old order is renewed with increased intensity. It is most significant that the Lord's violent action in the Jewish temple is set between the two halves of the story of the barren fig tree, which was destroyed because of its unfruitfulness. We are meant to see that Judaism itself is doomed; it cannot endure the revelation of the coming of the Son, that is, as we were taught by the Transfiguration, of the glory of God. The leaders and representatives of the old order are blind and deaf; from the allegory of the wicked husbandmen we learn that the only Son, sent last of all by the owner of the vineyard, has arrived and is among them; but they cannot recognize Him. Indeed, the only person in the

* It may be pointed out that this coming of the Lord to the capital is an event of supreme importance in Mark, who may have purposely left other visits of the Lord to Jerusalem unrecorded, in order to lay the greatest possible emphasis on this final visit. Since the general framework of Mark is retained in Matthew and Luke, no difficulty therefore should be felt about any apparent discrepancy between the synoptists and St. John in this matter.

† It is noticeable that St. Mark, unlike the other two synoptists, does not represent the acclamations as referring, personally and specifically, to the Lord and to Him only.

setting of these chapters who explicitly recognizes and calls Him Son of David is the blind beggar, Bartimaeus, *before* the arrival at the doomed capital, Jerusalem. But the evangelist is careful to remind us that the Lord's exaltation, or glory, advances *pari passu* with the rejection of Him by the rulers of His nation; in the allegory the wicked husbandmen work their will upon the only Son, and kill him; but the allegory is followed immediately by an appeal to scripture, and ends with the quotation, 'The stone which the builders rejected, the same is made the head of the corner; this was from the Lord, and it is marvellous in our eyes'.

I desire to defer until the last lecture the very important chapter 13, the so-called Little Apocalypse, and also the Passion narrative itself, especially as I hope we may find reason to think that they are vitally connected. I will therefore end this lecture by reminding you that we were led to discern in this gospel, as its leading theme, the doctrine of the crucified Messiah, and to suggest that St. Mark sets himself to deal particularly with the problems raised by this strange combination. The Messiahship is demonstrated, above all, by the divine testimony given to the Lord both at His baptism and at the Transfiguration; and it is exemplified also in His mighty works, so prominent in the first half of this gospel. But St. Mark's theme is also that of a crucified Messiah, and therefore he traces the course of events which led to the cross, and the origins and causes of the conflicts that arose between the Lord and the leaders of His nation. Incidentally, he shows that the Lord is innocent of any just charge, except the charge—immediately before the end—that He claimed to be Messiah. This claim, St. Mark emphasizes, was never put forward with dangerous insistence or in such a way as to justify a charge of sedition or of incitement of the people to disorder. Nor was the Lord hostile to the law of Moses; when He was asked to state the foremost commandment in the law, His answer, though perfectly adapted to express His own deepest convictions, is none the less orthodoxy itself; Israel's great confession with respect to God, combined with the kindred precept of love to a neighbour. Adequate and convincing proof is thus given that the Pharisees' conflicts with the Lord and, at the end, the Sadducees' plots against Him were in no way due to any sinister declaration on His part against the law of Moses.

The conflicts arose over the method of applying the law, over the Lord's understanding of its real purpose, and His perception of the ideals by the pursuit of which the loyal Jew should seek to fulfil the will of the God of Abraham, Isaac, and Jacob. St. Mark seeks to prove that the Lord met His death, not because His thought or His life ran counter to the law, but because He claimed to be the Messiah. It is perhaps significant, especially in view of such earlier passages in this gospel as 2^1 to 3^6, 7^{1-15}, 10^{1-12}, that at the examination before the Sanhedrin no charge is alleged of sabbath-breaking or of disobedience to the law, but only that of a threat to destroy—or, may we say, in the light of the sentence as a whole, to transform—the Temple.

It may be for the reasons which we have been considering, that St. Mark has told us so little about many things, a knowledge of which, we may be inclined to think, would have been of the greatest help and value to us; I touched upon some of them in the first lecture. The reason, put very briefly, is that he is using the traditional materials at his disposal with one leading purpose in mind. He is not interested in the Lord's biography as such; he is only interested in it, in so far as the traditions help him to set forth what he understands to be the Gospel. He also wishes to show, as subordinate themes, both how and why, when the fullness of the time came, the Jewish leaders not only failed to welcome their Messiah, but rejected and scorned Him, and therewith brought doom and ruin on themselves and on their nation. He strives to keep before his readers the vital connexion between the Lord's self-oblation on the cross, in obedience to His Father's will, and His might and glory, both in the works of mercy in the first half of the book and in the supreme moment of the Transfiguration. It is true that the evangelist has incidentally given us some most precious traits of the 'Jesus of history', to use a phrase now in common use, simply because he is still comparatively close to the actual facts. But probably we shall best understand his book and his purpose, if we regard both it and the little sections by means of which it is so largely built up, as an illustration, exposition and demonstration of the Church's Gospel.

IV

THE CONNEXION OF CHAPTER THIRTEEN
WITH THE PASSION NARRATIVE

IT will be remembered that, though St. Mark's gospel concerns itself chiefly with the Lord's actions, there are two chapters, four and thirteen, which are remarkable for the exceptional amount of teaching or discourse which they contain. When we considered the earlier of these two chapters, that is, Mark 4^{1-34}, I suggested that parables and sayings are recorded at this point, not so much in order to provide examples of the Lord's method of teaching and its content, as to give an assurance, in traditional sayings of the Lord which the evangelist found at his disposal, of the final, ultimate, certain success of His mission in spite of present, temporary difficulty and hindrance. In chapters 2 and 3 opposition to the Lord and His activities had already become pronounced; and accordingly in chapter 4 the reader is reminded, by means of a grouping together of parables and sayings of the Lord, that His cause will triumph. Probably the purpose of chapter 13 is largely similar, but now the horizon is far wider, and the surrounding darkness also very much greater. Chapter 13 is a great divine prophecy of the ultimate salvation of the elect after and indeed through unprecedented and unspeakable suffering, trouble, and disaster.

Throughout chapters 11 and 12, from the time of the arrival at Jerusalem, the reader has been made conscious of impending catastrophe. After the Lord's violent action in the Temple, we read, at 11^{18}, in language closely reminiscent of 3^6, 'the chief priests and the scribes sought how they might destroy him'. The incident of the withered fig tree suggests that the existing order of Judaism is doomed, and this interpretation is expressly confirmed by the allegory of the wicked husbandmen. From it we learn that if the husbandmen fill up the measure of their fathers and now proceed to kill the only Son, they will themselves be overwhelmed in ruin, and their vineyard forfeited. And finally we have the attempts of the various parties, Pharisees, Herodians, Sadducees, to entrap the Lord in talk. At 13^1

the Lord leaves the temple for the last time, and in reply to a disciple, who calls His attention to its grandeur and sublimity, He proclaims its coming utter destruction.

This last episode leads immediately to the long continuous discourse of thirty-two verses, which we are now to consider; and it will in turn be followed at once by the continuous Passion narrative in chapters 14 and 15. We notice also that from this point, 13¹, the ministry is over. The crowd which hitherto has been more or less consistently in evidence—it is mentioned twice in chapter 11, and three times in chapter 12—now disappears, to be heard only once more, in chapter 15, asking for Barabbas. Only disciples remain in the presence of the Lord, and to four only of these—to the leaders Peter, James, John, Andrew—is the discourse addressed, and it is expressly stated to be given in private.* The Lord is seated over against the temple on the Mount of Olives, which according to Zechariah 14⁴ is the destined scene of the apocalyptic judgement, and, as He speaks, He looks down across the valley on the doomed building, the heart of the religious life of Jewry.

The discourse itself falls into three parts:

> verses 5 to 13, the beginning of the consummation;
> verses 14 to 27, the consummation itself;
> verses 28 to 37, warnings in connexion with it.

The first part, verses 5 to 13, falls into two sections, each beginning with the warning, 'Take ye heed'. In the first section we read of internal religious distress, of external dangers, and of upheavals in the Gentile world; these things are said to be the beginning of the travail pangs of the consummation. In the second section we read of the grievous lot in store for disciples, and of the paramount necessity that they shall remain firm and steadfast.† This ends part 1.

The second part, verses 14 to 27, which deals with the actual consummation, falls into four sections of three sayings each.

---

* It is important that this feature of the discourse in Mark should be kept in mind, especially since in the corresponding discourse in Luke the note of privacy is pointedly omitted.

† For the sake of the analysis, verse 10, the concluding sentence of verse 11, and verse 13 have not been included here. They are said to disturb the otherwise poetic form of the strophes which we are considering. It will be noticed that each contains an assurance calculated to bring strength and help to those undergoing the trials which are described in each of the three parts of this second section.

The first section describes the beginning of the crisis in Jerusalem and Judaea; the second dwells on its terrible nature and duration; the third describes the coming of false Messiahs and false prophets; and in the fourth we hear of the dissolution of the natural order, the coming of the Son of man, and His summoning of His elect.

The third and last part of the discourse, verses 28 to 37, consists of warnings in connexion with the consummation, and of some other sayings more or less closely bearing on it, and the conclusion is reached with the reiterated command to watch, a command now explicitly addressed to all, and no longer only to the four immediate hearers.

A remarkable feature of the discourse is that it contains at least as much counsel and warning as apocalyptic revelation, these being combined in a way unusual in apocalyptic Jewish writings. We notice, for example, in part one, the way in which the second section of the first part, verses 9 to 13, a passage according to our present text* full of counsel and encouragement to disciples in their sufferings, follows immediately on the first section which deals solely and objectively with internal religious distress and external international upheavals. The chapter as a whole may be regarded as a farewell utterance of the Lord to His Church through His four most intimate disciples. This indeed is suggested by its closing words, 'What I say unto you I say unto all'. It is, I repeat, a great divine prophecy, delivered in private, of ultimate triumph through unspeakable and unprecedented horror and disaster.

It should be noticed that in this chapter there is no direct reference to the immediately imminent death of the speaker; and the divorce between chapter 13, the so-called apocalyptic chapter, and chapters 14 and 15, which form the Passion narrative, seems at first sight absolute; and you will remember my reference, in an earlier lecture, to the very big break which Westcott and Hort insert at this point between the paragraph which ends at 13[37] and that with which the Passion narrative begins at 14[1]. On the other hand, it would perhaps be generally agreed that chapter 13 is undoubtedly designed by the evangelist as the immediate introduction to the Passion narrative, in the sense that as we read the story of the Passion in this gospel in its

* See preceding note.

utter realism and unrelieved tragedy we are to remember always the person and office of Him of whom we read. He, who is now reviled, rejected, and condemned is none the less the supernatural Son of man; and the terrible story of the last twenty-four hours has for its other side that eternal weight of glory which was reached and could only be reached, as the Church believed, through the Lord's death upon the cross, and through the sufferings of His disciples also.*

This view of the relationship between chapter 13 on the one hand and chapters 14 and 15 on the other would perhaps, as I have said, meet with general acceptance; but recently a tendency has arisen to think that the relationship may be closer and more subtle than was previously supposed; and I desire now to lay this possibility before you.

There is a significant assertion in Hoskyns and Davey's great commentary upon the fourth gospel that, as a result of our study of that gospel, we ought to understand our earliest gospel, Mark, much better. To put the matter briefly and crudely, truths which are worked out fully in John may be discerned at an earlier stage, and in a less coherent form, in Mark. And it is undoubtedly the case that in the fourth gospel the exaltation of the Son of man is the moment when He is lifted up upon the cross; His glory is His self-oblation and self-revelation in the Passion; at that moment is the judgement of this world, and its prince, the devil, is overthrown, cast out. It is true that the idea of a future glory and a future judgement is not so entirely absent from the fourth gospel as is sometimes thought; but it is certainly a fact that the Lord's ministry, death and resurrection, and His subsequent commission of His disciples are regarded in John as providing almost all that we usually associate with the doctrines of His exaltation and His future coming.

Is it then possible that a comparison of certain passages in Mark 13 with others in Mark 14 and 15 will reveal an unexpected parallelism, however slight and tentative, between the apocalyptic prophecy and the Passion narrative?†

Let us notice, first, the use in both passages of the verb to hand up, or to deliver over. It occurs three times in chapter 13,

---

* Cf. Rom. 8^{17}.

† In the paragraph which follows, I am indebted to some suggestions made by the Rev. Dr. A. M. Farrer.

and ten times in chapters 14 and 15. It is almost always a word of sinister meaning in Mark,* implying the delivery of someone or something good to an evil power; thus it is the word regularly used of the action of Judas in handing over his Master to the Jewish authorities. In chapter 13 it is used, in all three cases, of the sufferings of members of the Church; let us consider the first of these, according to Professor C. H. Turner's punctuation of the passage, 13⁹. 'They shall deliver you up; in councils and synagogues ye shall be beaten; and ye shall stand before governors and kings.' The parallel with parts of 14⁵³ to 15¹⁵, the treatment of the Lord before the Jewish and the Gentile tribunals, is obvious and striking. The Lord is delivered by Judas to the Sanhedrin; he stands before it and before Pilate the governor, and He is scourged.

At 13²².²³ we read, 'There shall arise false Christs and false prophets, and shall shew signs and wonders, that they may lead astray, if possible, the elect. But take ye heed; behold, I have told you all things beforehand.' In the Passion narrative in Mark the action of Judas is foretold at the last supper; and on the way to Gethsemane the disciples are warned that they will all be caused to stumble. When Peter protests, he is told that for him an even greater fall is reserved. In the event, Judas delivers up his Master; all the disciples desert; and Peter denies Him. In other words, the disciples, the elect, were told all things beforehand; yet they were all led astray; only one, however, Judas, failed completely. I must be allowed to say dogmatically that in the fourth gospel Judas is probably 'the man of sin', the 'anti-Christ'.†

At 13³².³³ we read 'But of that day or that *hour* knoweth no one, not even the angels in heaven, neither the Son, but the Father. Take ye heed, watch and pray; for ye know not when the time is.'

Let us compare these verses closely with the scene in Gethsemane, as described in Mark. The Lord has withdrawn with the three, Peter, James, and John, and has asked them to share His vigil. He Himself then withdraws still farther, and alone, and prays that, if it be possible, the *hour* may pass away from Him; but He subordinates His wish absolutely to the will of

---

* The only possible exceptions are at 4²⁹ and 7¹³. It occurs elsewhere in this gospel eighteen times.

† Cf. John 17¹² and also 2 Thess. 2³.

His Father. Clearly the hour has not yet arrived in all its fullness; and there is a possibility that it may pass. Meantime, however, the three disciples three times fail to obey His request that they should also watch; and it may be that through their failure the Lord learns that His prayer will not be granted, that the hour has come and He is to bear it alone; and that Judas represents the anti-Christ—shall we say?—of the first advent. Thus the Lord in this matter now attains for the first time to the full, complete knowledge of the Father, and the scene ends with the half-reproachful words to the disciples who have failed Him, 'Sleep on now, and take your rest; it is enough; *the hour has come*; behold, the Son of man is delivered up into the hands of the sinners.* Arise, let us be going; behold, he that delivers me up has drawn near. And straightway, while he yet spake, cometh Judas.'

The question has often been asked why it seems to be assumed in 13^{35} that the coming of the Lord of the house will take place at night, and not by day. 'Watch therefore: for ye know not when the Lord of the house cometh, whether at even, or at midnight, or at cockcrowing, or in the morning; lest coming suddenly he find you sleeping.' Is it possible that there is here a tacit reference to the events of that supreme night before the Passion? On that *evening* the Lord *comes* for the last supper with the twelve; the scene in Gethsemane, and still more the arrest, which as we have just seen finally dates the arrival of 'the hour', would take place towards midnight; Peter denies the Lord at cockcrow; and '*in the morning* the chief priests with the elders and scribes, and the whole council, held a consultation, and bound Jesus, and carried him away, and *delivered him up* to Pilate'. In any case, it is very noticeable that in the Passion narrative of this gospel the last hours of the Lord's life are reckoned at three-hour intervals,† which is also the method adopted in 13^{35}—an exactness of temporal reckoning to which St. Mark is usually indeed a stranger.

---

* This verse may with some reason be described as the most terrible in Mark; for the expression 'the sinners' certainly includes a reference to the Gentiles, cf. Gal. 2^{15}. The third and last prophecy of the Passion was the first to state explicitly that the leaders of the Jewish nation would themselves hand over the Son of man, their lord and king, to the nations of the world, 10^{33}; this prophecy is now to be fulfilled forthwith.

† 14$^{68.72}$, 15$^{1.25.33.42}$.

Lastly, the verse 13²⁶, 'Then shall they see the Son of man coming in clouds with great power and glory' recalls at once 14⁶², the Lord's declaration to the Sanhedrin. 'The high priest asked him and saith unto him, Art thou the Messiah, the Son of God? And Jesus said, I am: and ye shall see the Son of man sitting at the right hand of power, and coming with the clouds of heaven.'* There is obviously a tacit identification of the Prisoner with the expected Son of man, whom one day every eye shall see as both Judge and Saviour, and the thought may be similar to that of the fourth gospel, where it is made clear that, if the Lord stands before judges, whether the Sanhedrin or Pilate, yet in reality it is He who is judge, not they; and possibly St. Mark's gospel may contain a hint of this. Certainly in Jewish thought one great purpose of the coming of the Son of man would be the judgement of the nations; and surprise has often been expressed that no reference to such judgement is made at 13²⁶, which describes the coming of the Son of man, but only to the gathering together of His elect. If, however, St. Mark's thought is partly fixed on the judgement effected, according to the thought of St. John's gospel, by the Passion of the Lord, this may account for the silence at 13²⁶ as regards the judgement of the nations of the world at the expected coming of the Son of man.

We have been seeking to trace certain parallelisms between the language and thought of chapter 13 and those of chapters 14 and 15. Obviously, if the parallelisms are in any way justified, then one verse in chapter 13, 13³⁰, becomes much less difficult than is usually supposed. 'Verily I say unto you, this generation shall not pass away, until all these things be accomplished.' A first fulfilment at any rate was not far off, which was itself regarded as a sign, a seal or assurance, and a sacrament of the ultimate fulfilment.

It may be worthy of remark that the most striking parallelisms between chapter 13 and the Passion narrative occur either in the third part of the discourse in chapter 13, that part which, as we saw, consists chiefly of warnings to watchfulness on the part of the disciples and may be, more than the rest of the discourse, a collection of originally separate sayings, or, if in

---

* On the high priest's lips 'the Blessed' is a periphrasis for 'God', in order to avoid the actual mention of the divine name; similarly 'power', in the next line.

the earlier parts, in those which deal particularly with the sufferings of disciples. The arrival of the hour, the Lord's Passion, and the sufferings and endurance of His Church are linked indissolubly together.

In chapters 14 and 15 St. Mark relates the story of the Passion in very simple but dignified language; only towards the climax of the narrative do the sentences become short and terse, as though the tension were near breaking-point. Echoes of the fulfilment of Old Testament prophecies are constantly heard; they are recognized to some extent by all, and I need not stop to dwell upon them. The story is, upon the whole, allowed to speak for itself; but the evangelist emphasizes strongly certain features, which may help to show us what he chiefly has in mind. In the first place, he is at particular pains to dwell upon the steadily increasing and finally complete dereliction of the Lord. The chief priests plot; one of the twelve plays into their hands, and delivers up his Master; the rest of the disciples desert, and their leader Peter disowns; the council of the nation condemns the Son of man Himself, and He is delivered to the Gentile power; finally, the sense of His Father's presence is withdrawn. We may miss the significance of this emphasis on the dereliction, more strongly stressed in Mark than in any other gospel, unless we contrast it continually with the work and achievements of the Lord in the first half of the book. He who there in the fullness of His power diffuses health and light and life is here seen in uttermost abandonment; He who once proclaimed that all things were possible to faith and courage is now seen tied and bound and helpless; but it is the same Person in each case; indeed, His past work and also, as the evangelist and his readers were well aware, His future power to help depend upon His present state.

Secondly, it is hardly possible in my opinion to exaggerate the significance of the abrupt and astonishing verse 15[38], 'The veil of the temple was rent in two [torn asunder] from the top to the bottom'. These words occur immediately after the record of the Lord's death, and before the comment of the Roman centurion, at the foot of the cross, upon that death. For a single instant, therefore, we are transplanted from Golgotha to the Temple area, and then back again to Golgotha. Surely it is only familiarity which conceals from us the strangeness and also the significance of St. Mark's record at this point. I must be allowed to state my belief, without pausing to try to justify it, that the reference in this verse is to the veil which the writer of the epistle to the Hebrews* calls the second veil, that is, the veil in front of the tabernacle called The Holy of Holies, concealing the very presence of God.† If so, St. Mark thus seems to wish to teach us that by the fact and at the moment of the Lord's death the barrier which had hitherto existed between God and man, a barrier so strongly emphasized in Jewish religion, has been broken down. It is not likely to be accidental that the Greek verb for to rend occurs in Mark only in two places. At the baptism we read that, as the Lord ascended from the waters of Jordan, He saw the heavens rending asunder and the divine presence descending upon Him like a dove. This, I suggested, is St. Mark's description of the incarnation, in and by which heaven and earth were joined in an irrevocable, unbreakable union. The other passage in which this verb is used is the verse we are now considering. As the earlier verse described the incarnation, when in the person of the Lord heaven descended to earth, so this verse, coming immediately after the death of the Lord, describes the at-one-ment between God and man, which He by His death has thus effected. In Him earth has now been raised to heaven, and in the light of His death is seen the meaning of the imperfect and partial relations which existed between God and man under the old covenant; these now attain their completion or fulfilment.

We may consider the same truth, if we use a different avenue of approach, and pass, in the third place, to the next verse, 15³⁹, which records the comment of the Roman centurion, 'Truly this man was Son of God', or perhaps, a son of God. For our present purpose it is not necessary to try to decide whether the evangelist understood these words to have been spoken in mockery, or as a genuine confession. If, on the one hand, they were spoken in mockery, they merely fall into line with the other mocking titles, such as the Messiah, or the King of Israel, given to the Lord beneath the cross, titles, however, which the reader knows

---

* Hebrews 9³. The following passages of this epistle should also be consulted: 9⁷ ᶠ. ²⁴⁻⁸, 10¹⁹ ᶠ..

† We may compare Isa. 45¹⁵: 'Verily thou art a God that hidest thyself, O God of Israel, the Saviour.'

to be in fact correct. If, on the other hand, as I should myself incline to think, St. Mark wishes us to understand the words as a genuine confession, the centurion represents, as it were, the first-fruits of the Gentiles unto Christ. In either case, the expression Son of God recalls to the reader two momentous earlier occasions in this gospel when the Lord has received this same title, only then in the form beloved, or only, Son of God. He is thus addressed when He first comes upon the scene in this gospel, in the story of the baptism; and in what we may call the central panel of the book, the Transfiguration, He is thus revealed in all the glory and majesty of that unique Sonship to the three leaders of the twelve. Apart from two confessions by demons in chapters 3 and 5 respectively, and 12^6 where the term is also applied to Him, indirectly, in the allegory of the wicked husbandmen, these three passages, the baptism, the Transfiguration, and the centurion's confession, are the only three occasions in Mark when the divine Sonship is directly ascribed to the Lord; and it is probably no accident that they occur at the beginning, in the middle, and at the close of the book. The reader is thus reminded that He who has just died is the only, or beloved, Son of God. We have to ask, what is the importance of His unique Sonship in connexion with His death, and once more we are driven back, as in the consideration of the term the Son of man, to a consideration of certain features in the earlier covenant.

In this it is a fundamental conception that the first-born in Israel belong to the Lord; and if not offered in sacrifice to Him, they must be redeemed. The story of Abraham's sacrifice of Isaac illustrates this conception very clearly, and it is remarkable that in this story, in the Septuagint translation of the Hebrew, Isaac is three times referred to as the only son, the term used, as we have seen, of the divine Sonship of Jesus Christ in Mark 1^{11} and 9^7, and again, indirectly, in the allegory of the wicked husbandmen, at 12^6. In the story of Abraham and Isaac, however, the only son is in the end not required in sacrifice; a ram is offered and accepted in his stead. The feature of the new covenant which moved St. Paul* so strongly was that in the new dispensation God did *not* spare His only Son; no substitute was possible; the only Son was offered, and Himself accepted

* See, for example, Rom. 8^{32}.

the office laid upon Him, as St. Mark's story of Gethsemane makes clear. Here therefore the only Son fills the part, not of Isaac, but of the ram; and thereby those for whom He offers Himself now find themselves in the position of Isaac; although utterly unworthy, they, like Isaac, are redeemed, accepted through the offering of Another. It seems probable that St. Mark is reminding his readers of this truth, when he thus records the centurion's utterance immediately after the Lord's death, apart from the single verse about the rending of the veil. There is surely no need here for the distinctive term only Son, which would presumably have been unnatural on the lips of a Roman centurion; the reference to divine sonship is enough. 'When the centurion, which stood by over against him, saw that he so breathed out his life, he said, Truly this man was Son of God'. Does St. Mark wish us to see, that with that breathing out of His life the perfect offering has been made, and man is reconciled to God?*

If the considerations which have been before us in these lectures are on the whole well grounded, the treatment which St. Mark's gospel seems to have received throughout the centuries may not unnaturally surprise us. Those who believe that it was used by both St. Matthew and St. Luke may feel that at the outset these evangelists laid very violent hands upon it; and the origin of the keen interest which, for the first time so far as we know, it began to arouse in the last century, was a discovery with no religious basis but due solely to a literary

---

* Dr. C. H. Dodd, in the broadcast address which will be quoted on p. 89, thinks that the centurion is most likely to have connected the term 'son of God' with the Emperor whom he served. 'It expressed', says Dr. Dodd, 'the subject peoples' sense of the majesty and power of Rome, embodied in the supernatural person of the Emperor. For a soldier to give this title to a Jew whom he had seen condemned and put to death meant a surprising change of mind. It meant not only that he had changed his mind about Jesus, but that he had begun to change his mind about God, or at least about what was really divine. He had been brought up to think that the most divine thing on earth was the splendour and military might of Rome and Caesar. Now he had somehow an inkling that divinity might reside where there was no visible might or splendour. All that was here was sheer goodness, fortitude, and self-sacrifice; and yet he saw a 'son of God'. The veil, Mark said, was rent; God stood revealed. The first witness to it is this pagan soldier, who sees divinity where he had least expected to see it.'

I am glad to call attention to this striking interpretation of the passage, but I should be sorry to give up the connexion of the term, as used here, with its previous use or the use of synonyms for it in this gospel; and on Dr. Dodd's interpretation this would presumably be necessary.

comparison of the first three gospels, and the consequent realization that St. Mark was probably our earliest evangelist. Between these two periods this gospel seems, in comparison with its peers, to have been almost continuously neglected. No doubt it is true that the hopes which were aroused by the discovery of its temporal priority have not been in all cases fully realized; at first, owing to the dominant interests of the time, a burden was laid upon the book which we now realize is more than it can bear; but on other and more permanent grounds we may well come to be increasingly thankful that the wisdom of the Church was guided to grant a place to St. Mark's work within its fourfold Gospel.

V

THE CLEANSING OF THE TEMPLE
IN ST. MARK'S GOSPEL

AT first sight St. Mark's story of the cleansing of the temple by the Lord on his arrival at Jerusalem shortly before the Passion seems to be easily intelligible and to present fewer problems than many others in this gospel. It is true that it has some remarkable features which have often been pointed out: thus it is the only act of violence recorded of the Lord; and surprise has been expressed that St. Mark does not relate any immediate counter-action on the part of the temple authorities, such as occurred forthwith, after St. Peter had healed a lame man in the same vicinity, Acts 4[1]; but otherwise most hearers or readers of the story to-day probably interpret it without difficulty along the following lines. On the Lord's arrival at the temple, His indignation is aroused when He sees that commerce and traffic in the sacrificial animals is allowed within the temple precinct and that in consequence the atmosphere of peace and solemnity befitting the temple area is endangered. He forthwith carries through a drastic purgation of the court affected, and justifies His action by recalling the prophecy of Isaiah 56[7], 'My house shall be called a house of prayer for all the nations', adding, with a pointed reference to a word of Jeremiah, 7[11], 'but ye have made it a den of thieves'. His action frightens the temple authorities, and they plot to kill Him. It may be questioned, however, whether such an interpretation is not too 'modern' and also too superficial in character to explain its important position in the Marcan gospel. As I wish to try to show, the cleansing is, according to St. Mark, the great act of the Lord as the messianic king on His arrival at His Father's house; was then His motive, in so acting, simply that of a puritan reformer, and further, had His energy and zeal, so far as we know, no further or deeper results?

It is a merit of the more recent study of St. Mark's gospel that, although we are bidden to regard each of his stories as a unit, with its own lesson and significance, we are encouraged also to seek traces of method in the evangelist's arrangement of the stories, and, above all, to find a connected narrative in his account of the Passion. His Passion narrative is usually regarded as beginning at 14^1, and not unnaturally, for chapter 13 is the so-called Little Apocalypse, and the greater part of chapter 12 is mainly occupied with questions put to or by the Lord. These two chapters, 12 and 13, break the connexion between chapter 11 and chapters 14 to 16. But it is worth consideration whether at an earlier stage of the tradition the entry into Jerusalem and the cleansing which follows it may not perhaps have been vitally connected, and have formed the immediate introduction to the Passion narrative; certainly, as we have already noticed, it is, according to St. Mark, the cleansing which causes the chief priests and the scribes to plan the Lord's death—11^{18}, 'And the chief priests and the scribes heard it, and sought how they might destroy him'—; and 14^1, usually regarded as an altogether fresh start, only repeats this decision, without fresh reason given —'And it was the passover and the unleavened bread after two days; and the chief priests and the scribes sought how they might take him by subtilty and kill him'.

But if the cleansing forms part of or is at least an introduction to the Passion narrative, then we must also add the Lord's entry into the city. Those who are learned in Eastern religious ceremonies say that such an event as the festal procession in 11$^{1-10}$ could only end at the temple. It is true that, according to St. Mark, unlike St. Matthew, the cleansing is separated by one day from the entry; but if St. Mark wished, in accordance with a method which he uses not infrequently elsewhere, to put the cleansing between the two parts of the withered fig-tree story, then he was bound to make a break, however slight, between the procession and the cleansing. According to St. Mark the Lord visits the temple after His entry into the city and looks round on all things before going out to Bethany; but He does not act until the next day, on His return in the morning to the city.

If these suggestions are on the right lines and there is a vital connexion between the procession into Zion, the cleansing of the temple, and the Passion, let us recall that in Mark, as indeed also in Matthew and Luke, this is the only coming of the Lord to Jerusalem during his ministry, and he comes, for those who have eyes to see, as its messianic king. In whatever way the evangelist may have wished his readers to interpret the acclamations recorded by him as having been uttered during the entry, he must have meant them to understand, in view of his previous narrative of Caesarea Philippi, that for disciples at any rate those acclamations were of a messianic character; the king has come to Zion; and the difficult phrase with which the acclamations end in Mark, Hosanna in the highest, is perhaps best interpreted as an appeal for divine help in the light of the Lord's messianic arrival.*

Let us now consider the circumstances of the cleansing in detail. It seems to be agreed that its scene was the so-called court of the Gentiles or heathen. This court was separated by a high partition-wall from the holier parts of the temple and is said to have had little sacred significance itself; at most, that of a very wide enclosure giving access to the interior parts of the building. It is true that this fore-court was actually part of the temple, and was protected, we are told, by certain regulations; thus no one was to pass through it with dusty feet or to use it as a thoroughfare; and the use of it was forbidden to the sick. But for convenience sake the temple authorities allowed the sacrificial beasts to be sold in this space, which was of very considerable size, and the Roman coins of the worshippers were exchanged here for the temple shekels, in which alone the annual tribute to the temple and payments for the sacrificial traffic could be made. This arrangement may no doubt have been a source of profit to the ecclesiastics, but assuredly also it was of the greatest assistance to Jewish pilgrims from both near and far.

* The Hebrew word Hosanna, here transliterated into Greek, seems to be a festal appeal for divine help, and may be interpreted as meaning, 'May God save Israel'. It occurs at Psalm 118²⁵, and in the LXX is there translated as 'Save now', elsewhere as 'give help'. In the present context, Mark 11⁹ ᶠ·, as also at Matt. 21⁹, it is repeated at the end of the cry with the difficult addition 'in the highest'. The Greek word, translated highest, occurs thirteen times in the New Testament. In nine of these cases it is an equivalent for or an epithet of the transcendent God, e.g. Acts 7⁴⁸. Of the remaining four cases, three occur at this point in the three synoptic gospels; and the other is at Luke 2¹⁴, where the expression 'in the highest' is clearly antithetical to 'on the earth'. In Psalm 148¹, 'in the heights' 1ᵇ is obviously equivalent to 'from the heavens' 1ᵃ, both phrases being opposed to 'from the earth', verse 7. We may therefore reasonably suppose that the last words of the cry, as recorded in Mark and Matthew, may mean, 'May God save Israel from heaven', i.e. by His own unique act, by some transcendent action; cf. Luke 1⁷⁸. It was indeed an accepted Jewish belief that *God* would bring the kingdom.

This interpretation seems at least more suitable than Prof. F. C. Burkitt's explanation, 'Up with your green boughs' (*Jesus Christ, an historical outline*, p. 43).

As regards the interior parts of the temple, devoted to Jewish sacrifice and Jewish worship, the Lord, it seems, found no fault, or at any rate did not intervene; on the other hand he appears to charge the authorities with the desecration of the whole building owing to the traffic which they permitted in this outer court.

According to all three synoptists the Lord appeals, in support of his action, to the prophetic word 'My house shall be called a house of prayer', St. Mark alone completing the sentence, as it is found in Isaiah, with the words 'for all the nations'. The prophecy itself stands in the midst of promises which describe Yahweh's generous purposes both for his own people, the Jews, and for all peoples:

Also the strangers, that join themselves to the Lord, to minister unto him, and to love the name of the Lord, to be his servants, every one that keepeth the sabbath from profaning it, and holdeth fast by my covenant; even them will I bring to my holy mountain, and make them joyful in my house of prayer; their burnt offerings and their sacrifices shall be accepted upon mine altar: for mine house shall be called an house of prayer for all peoples. The Lord God which gathereth the outcasts of Israel saith, Yet will I gather others to him, beside his own that are gathered.

It will be noticed that the prophet speaks, not of a present order of things, not of a present temple-dispensation, but of a destiny and function designed by Yahweh for the house of his good pleasure. The present order, that of the prophet's own day, when the temple was not yet a house of prayer for all the nations, had indeed its divinely ordered functions; but since the Jew always and inevitably looked forward—his goal was always in a future not manifest as yet—the order of the temple service, as the prophet knew it, could not be final; according to him the Jewish temple would one day, when the messianic age arrived, become a house of prayer not only for the Jews but for all the nations.

If this view is correct, it is noticeable that the prophecy and the Lord's action are both concerned with the rights and privileges of Gentiles. No attempt is made to interfere with the existing Jewish ritual or worship, and the Lord confines himself entirely to the removal, from the court of the Gentiles, of all that made prayer or worship difficult or impossible for Gentiles, in that one and only part of the temple to which they had already the privilege of access.

The existence of a court for the Gentiles in this area, in the very heart of Judaism, is indeed remarkable. It is due to the belief, found frequently in the Old Testament, that the Jewish ordinance and worship is the only true form and method of the adoration of God, in combination with another belief, less often found indeed in the Old Testament but unquestionably present there, that one day all the nations would be partakers in this worship.* There is reason to think that both the Jewish claim to possess the only true worship of God and the Jewish hope that one day all the nations would join in this worship were not prominent in Jewish thought generally at the beginning of our era, although to the mind of a man like St. Paul they may no doubt have presented, before his conversion, a heart-searching problem.† If so, the Lord's action, apart from its astonishing character, may not have seemed to the passer-by of any supreme religious significance or importance at the time. But in the light of the context in Mark it assumes a momentous character. For even before the arrival of the messianic king the Gentiles had been allowed certain privileges upon the threshold of the temple, and of these the Jewish authorities, according to the Lord's word in Mark, had allowed them to be robbed; must it not therefore be the first act of the messianic king on his arrival to restore to Gentiles at least those religious rights and privileges which ought already to be theirs, especially if, as would surely happen with the coming of Messiah, Jewish worship would now become a universal worship? In the Lord's action therefore, as described in Mark, we see Him concerned, not with any problems or practices of the existing Jewish wor-

---

* The thought of Jerusalem as mother of the nations is prominent in Psalm 87; and the following rabbinical lines which may be of the fourth century A.D. (Midrash Tanchuma, ed. Choreb, p. 444, 15–18) illustrate the same idea in Ezekiel 5⁵:

The land of Israel lies in the middle of the world,
Jerusalem „ „ the land of Israel,
The holy precinct „ „ Jerusalem,
The temple „ „ the holy precinct,
The ark of the covenant „ the temple,
The foundation-stone lies before the ark of the covenant,
For from it did the foundation of the world proceed.

† On this point there is a valuable passage in R. H. Hutton's *Theological Essays*, pp. 318–27.

ship in the temple, but with the position of the Gentile nations in respect of their worship of the one true God.

This raises the problem of the Lord's relation, during His ministry, to the Gentiles; it is a problem which meets us constantly in the study of the gospels, and admits of no easy, quick solution. In Matthew, for example, on the occasion of the mission of the Twelve, we find the injunction 'Go not into any way of the Gentiles'; but against it we may set, from the same gospel, 'Many shall come from the east and the west, and shall sit down with Abraham and Isaac and Jacob in the kingdom of heaven'. In Mark we have the Galilean ministry, obviously directed chiefly to Jews, and the feeding of the multitude in Galilee; but against these we find the withdrawal to the north and east, and the feeding of the multitude in Decapolis. Probably we come nearest to a solution, particularly of the problem as it is laid before us in St. Matthew's gospel, if we recall the words at the last supper about the blood of the covenant poured out for *many*. It is the Lord's death which is to change the status of the Gentiles in relation to the Jews, and indeed to Yahweh Himself. In the word 'many' there is unquestionably a reminiscence of the great servant-passage in Isaiah 53, and some of our best guides tell us that 'many' here does not mean 'some' as against 'all', but on the contrary 'all' as against 'one'; the Lord, who is speaking, stands alone, on one side, and many, that is, all, upon the other side; so that the word 'many' includes a reference to the Gentiles, indeed, it may be, has them especially in mind.

Again, we may recall, in our consideration of this matter, that in the last words of St. Matthew's gospel the disciples are expressly bidden to evangelize 'all the nations', the very expression used in the quotation from Isaiah in Mark, on the occasion of the cleansing of the temple. The contrast in Matthew between the words in 28[19] and those in 10[5] is remarkable; but the reason is plain; it is the Lord's atoning death and resurrection which renders possible the universalization, the catholicizing, of His work and message.

Indeed, it may be for this reason that St. Matthew in his narrative of the cleansing, though doubtless he had Mark's quotation in its fullness before him, omits the last four English words at this point, reserving for Matthew 28[19] the reference to 'all the nations'. Just as, in his account of the Baptist's work, when he comes to Mark's description of the Baptist 'proclaiming a baptism of repentance with a view to remission of sins', he carefully omits at this point the last seven English words, lest they should involve misunderstanding, and reserves them for an addition to the Marcan rendering of the Lord's words at the Last Supper, 'This is my blood of the covenant which is poured forth for many'; so here, although in full sympathy, as we have every reason to believe, with St. Mark's interpretation of the cleansing, he carefully reserves the express reference to the Gentiles for the last message of the Lord to the eleven, *after* His death and resurrection. Certainly St. Matthew is always careful to ensure, as far as may be, that there shall be no doubt about his meaning, doctrinally or otherwise. Opportunity may be taken to illustrate this habit of the first evangelist by a consideration of two remarkable additions which he makes to the Marcan account of the cleansing of the temple. He adds, first, that blind and lame folk came to the Lord in the temple and He healed them; and secondly, that the children greeted Him with the cry 'Hosanna to the son of David'. (This expression may present difficulty to the Hebraist, but at any rate the triumphant significance ascribed to the words by the evangelist is clear.) Are not these two features of St. Matthew's record probably the method which he adopts of emphasizing the messianic significance of the Lord's action in the cleansing? Is it possible that in the mention of the blind and the lame he is thinking symbolically of the Gentiles?

Perhaps then St. Mark wishes his readers to draw the same lesson from the cleansing as from the Lord's words at the Last Supper. On each occasion the Lord, as interpreted to us by St. Mark and St. Matthew, is concerned with one particular aspect of the arrival of the messianic age, as foreseen here and there in the Old Testament, namely, the universalization of the Jewish worship of God. We may express the truth which we are trying to express, first, in general terms. The Lord's life seems to have been spent almost entirely among His own people, and His mission to have been directed almost solely to them; but none the less, as a result of His life and mission within Judaism, all the ends of the world are to see the salvation of God. Or we may consider the particular event which forms the subject of this paper. The arrival of the messianic king at his capital, and his action in its very heart, the temple area, is to benefit, above all, the non-Jewish peoples of the world.

It was remarked, a moment ago, that the Lord's action did not concern itself with that which would at once occur to the mind of every Jew as forming the most vital and important feature of the temple, namely, the appointed daily sacrifices and the ceaseless service of the priests. And yet, if we are right in regarding the cleansing as a sign or token that with the Lord's arrival at Jerusalem the messianic age, indeed the kingdom of God, was at the doors, then His action was certainly also concerned, even if only indirectly, with the Jewish ordinances. For these, though no doubt Yahweh's gifts to the people of His choice, were ordained, like all things Jewish, for the period *preceding* the end or consummation. In the end sacrifice and priesthood would cease, and if we may judge from the very Jewish book of Revelation, the Apocalypse, the whole nation would be a kingdom of priests.

Again, the Lord's action takes no account of the overwhelming secular power, the Roman colossus, vividly represented by the Turris Antonia, overlooking the temple. Both these authorities, the divinely given *temporal* authority of Jewish worship, and the world-embracing all-powerful secular authority of Rome, pale before the infinitely greater authority, revealed in the Lord's purification of the outer court of the Gentiles; for His action, resting on prophetic assurance, signifies, implies the imminent arrival of the *end*; and in that day, as the writers of the Old Testament knew well, nothing can survive in its own right. And yet, as the Lord's preparatory action shows, the arrival of that day is to unite in one the Jewish nation and the nations of the world; and His action takes place on hallowed ground, which hitherto has been almost though not quite exclusively reserved for Jewish sacrifice and priesthood.

Perhaps these reflections may help to explain the two difficulties which we mentioned at the outset; namely, that the cleansing is the only recorded act of violence by the Lord; and secondly, that St. Mark gives no account of any immediate reaction or counter-measures on the part of the authorities. He records indeed that in consequence they plan measures to destroy Him, and he thus brings the Lord's work on behalf of the Gentiles into closest connexion with His death; but the only immediate external result mentioned by St. Mark is the question, which 'the chief priests and the scribes and the elders' raise next day, of the Lord's authority and its origins.

Let us deal first with this second difficulty. Why does St. Mark give us no conclusion to the story of the cleansing or tell us how the rest of the day, after this remarkable event, was passed? Why does he concentrate our attention only on the question put on the next day about it to the Lord?

If we try to place ourselves in the position of the first and largely Gentile readers of St. Mark's gospel, is it not likely that for them the interest and significance of the Lord's action would centre in the removal by the Lord of the barrier which prevented the temple from being, according to its full destiny, a house of prayer for all the nations? In the eyes of the readers of this gospel, therefore, as they looked back on the astonishing events of the thirty years or more since the act itself took place, is not the cleansing likely to have appeared in the highest degree messianic or, to use a modern word, eschatological; and does it not become suitable and fitting that its importance should be shown by the question of the origin or ground of the Lord's authority in acting thus? The Lord, it will be remembered, declines to give an answer on this point, unless His questioners first admit the divine mission of the Baptist; and we recall that in St. Mark's gospel John the Baptist is indeed and most emphatically Elijah, the immediate herald of the end.

It remains to consider the cleansing as forming the only act of violence recorded of the Lord. True; but the action itself is fully in accord with His constant attitude towards several Jewish rites and customs. Thus it is a firm feature of the primitive tradition that the Lord was, on occasion, indifferent to ritual purity, to sabbath observance, and to fasting; and that He placed charity on a higher level than sacrifice. In all these matters, as in the cleansing itself, He displays essentially the characteristics of a prophet; and we may recall Dr. Wheeler Robinson's constant emphasis on the importance of the symbolic *actions* of the prophets as well as of their words. The action of a prophet, and that which his action symbolized, were vitally connected. And certainly St. John, in his account of the cleansing, regards it as 'a sign', in the Johannine sense, of the coming destruction of the temple, as well as of the Lord's own death, by which, in the fourth gospel, is given the full and complete revelation of God.*

* It will have been noticed that no account has been taken in this chapter of St. Luke's story of the cleansing. The reason is that the significance of the cleansing in his gospel is markedly different from that in the other three, for on this point we may place the fourth gospel alongside Matthew and Mark. St. Luke's account of the cleansing is extremely brief and is overshadowed by the lament over Jerusalem, which is placed between the procession into the city and the cleansing; nor is the question of the Lord's authority brought into close connexion with His action in the cleansing; in Luke 20$^{1f.}$ the expression 'these things' need not necessarily refer to the cleansing, as it must in Matthew and Mark and, we may add, in John. This deviation of St. Luke from the other evangelists is characteristic, and parallels to his method here could be given from other passages in his gospel. The probable explanation, put very briefly, is that part of his purpose is to lay a reduced emphasis on the very strongly eschatological element in the Gospel.

VI

THE CLEANSING OF THE TEMPLE
IN ST. JOHN'S GOSPEL

I

A N important feature of St. John's gospel is the part taken in the record by the Jews, particularly in their relation to the Lord. The frequent occurrence of the expression in this gospel is itself remarkable, as is readily seen, if we compare St. John's usage with that of the other evangelists. In the synoptists, if we disregard the title 'the King of the Jews', the expression 'the Jews' is found only four times altogether. It occurs in the editorial notes Mark $7^{3 f.}$* and Matthew 28^{15},† and also, quite naturally, in Luke 7^3, where the Roman centurion, himself a Gentile, sends to the Lord 'elders of the Jews'; and lastly in Luke 23^{51} where Joseph is described as 'of Arimathæa, a city of the Jews'. The absence of the expression in general is what we should expect, since the Lord Himself was born of Jewish lineage and worked almost entirely within the confines of Judaism. Who to-day, if describing political controversies in which Lord Salisbury or Mr. Gladstone was engaged in the latter part of the last century, would think it natural to say, 'The Prime Minister said to the British people', or the like? Would not the reference be to certain sections of the nation, such as the Conservatives or the Liberals or the Irish party, just as we find mention of Pharisees, Sadducees, and Herodians in the synoptic gospels? In St. John's gospel, however, after omitting, as in the case of the synoptists, all references to 'the King of the Jews', we find that the expression occurs more than fifty times. Occasionally, no doubt, the words, as in the synoptists, are in editorial contexts; examples of this usage are 4^9‡ and 19^{40}.§ But the most frequent use of the expression is *within* the course of the narrative itself; and usually it is 'the Jews' who engage in discussion or controversy with the Lord.‖

---

* 'The Pharisees, and all the Jews . . . eat not, holding the tradition of the elders.'
† 'This saying was spread abroad among the Jews, *and continueth* until this day.'
‡ 'For Jews have no dealings with Samaritans', but see R.V. mg.
§ 'As the custom of the Jews is to bury.'
‖ In a full and valuable note in the *Expository Times*, July 1949, the Rev. G. J.

We are led therefore to consider what the attitude of the evangelist is towards the Jews and Judaism in general, and here a careful distinction must be made between the Judaism of the past, and the Judaism, represented by 'the Jews', with which the Lord during His ministry is confronted in this gospel.

For the historic Judaism of the past, and for the Old Testament scriptures, St. John has nothing but respect. Thus salvation proceeds from the Jews (4^{22}); the Jewish temple is 'my Father's house'; to be called 'an Israelite indeed' is high praise (1^{47}); the Old Testament is reverenced (5^{46}, 10^{35}*) and a knowledge of its contents is assumed from the outset (1^{21-25}); but none the less in this book the Jews of the Lord's own day are, as such, not only always in the wrong but also the enemy from first to last; even those addressed at 8^{31}† are said at 8^{44} to be of their father the devil. And just as the scheme of St. Luke's gospel is to a large extent decided by its emphasis on the universalism of the Christian message, and that of St. Matthew's gospel by its emphasis on the new law and righteousness revealed by Christ, so the scheme of St. John's gospel is largely determined by the opposition between the Jews and the person of the Lord. And by this opposition they are shown to have chosen darkness, not light. Though the evangelist himself is almost certainly by origin a Jew, his attitude to Judaism is completely external.

II

We proceed to ask whether we can gain any light upon the significance seen by the evangelist in the cleansing of the Jewish temple by the Lord, and upon the position which he assigns to it in his narrative; and for this purpose it will be sufficient to consider in outline the contents and arrangement of the book as far as 4^{26}.

We need not linger over the introduction (1^{1-18}), except to

Cuming points out that 'the Jews' in St. John's gospel are usually not the Jewish nation as a whole, but those connected with Jerusalem, especially the chief priests and the Pharisees, and that the term almost always refers to Judaeans as opposed to Galileans. An interesting note on the point will also be found in Bernard's 'St. John', *I.C.C.* i. 34. Mr. Cuming further points out that similarly, in the seven contexts where St. John speaks of Judaea, he always means the southern region, as contrasted with Galilee, and never the whole of Palestine.

* 'Moses . . . wrote of me.' 'The scripture cannot be broken.'

† 'Jesus . . . said to those Jews which had believed him.'

remark that in 1¹⁷, where the Lord is mentioned for the first time by name, a sharp contrast is drawn between His work and that of Moses. This verse alone is sufficient to justify us in speaking of the old order or dispensation given through Moses, and the new order or dispensation inaugurated through Jesus Christ.

In the rest of chapter 1, which should probably be regarded as still preparatory to the ministry itself, witness is given by the forerunner, John, both to the unique nature of his successor and also to the office of the latter as the Lamb of God who lifts and takes away the sin of the world. Next, the Lord Himself invites certain men into His company, including Andrew's brother Simon, who forthwith receives the promise of his new name Peter, that is, Rock or Stone. These men in turn add their witness to that already given by John, for they ascribe to the Lord various messianic titles, which suggest that they already see in Him the fulfilment of the hope of Israel. And finally, in the last verse of chapter 1, the Lord Himself utters a solemn promise assuring His disciples that they are to be allowed to see the unveiling of heaven itself in the unbroken intercourse between His Father and Himself, the Son of man.* That which their Jewish forefather Jacob had seen long ago in his *dream* at Bethel is now to be realized, no longer as a hope or aspiration, but in *fact*. And the promise is to be realized in the coming ministry, not in some distant future.

If this is correct, with chapter 2 the promise given in 1⁵¹ begins to be fulfilled forthwith,† and the ministry opens with the presence of the Lord and His disciples at a wedding feast, appropriately enough, since elsewhere‡ He compares Himself and His disciples to a bridegroom and a bridegroom's fellows. There can be little doubt that the evangelist valued this story, the first significant action, as he himself is careful to note, in the record of the ministry, partly at any rate for its symbolical teaching. For it tells of water placed in stone waterpots which were connected with Jewish methods of purification, and how this same water, under the influence of the Lord, becomes wine of a surpassing quality. It thus sets forth, for him who is willing

---

* Cf. 15¹⁵, 'All things that I heard from my Father I have made known unto you'.

† Cf. 2¹¹, 'This beginning of his signs did Jesus in Cana of Galilee, and manifested forth his glory'.

‡ Mk. 2¹⁹, 'Can the sons of the bride-chamber fast, while the bridegroom is with them?'

so to read it, the relation of the old and the new order, and in a positive form; the latter is the perfecting and transformation of the former; with the arrival of the Son of man, the water of the Law becomes the wine of the Gospel. And we notice, lastly, that this *positive* work is achieved by Him *in Galilee*.

From Galilee we pass to Jerusalem, the centre of Jewish activity and life; but since we are to consider the story of the Lord's action in the temple more fully in a moment, let us at present only note three points about it. First, the Lord's activity is now revealed *at Jerusalem* in a *negative* way. The new order is seen here not as the gracious and perfect completion of the old order, but in opposition to it, and in some measure as its overthrow. Secondly, the Lord now comes for the first time in this gospel into direct contact with 'the Jews'. And thirdly, the story contains references to the Lord's death, indirectly in 2$^{17.\ 19}$, and directly in the explanation or interpretation given by the editorial notes in 2$^{21\ f.}$

Thus in 1$^{19-51}$ we have had the work and witness of John, and have been shown the foundation and the beginnings of the new community, together with the promise given to it in 1^{51}; and in chapter 2 we have seen the new order in action both positively and negatively. The questions now arise, what is the nature of this new order, and how is admission gained to it? and further, since the religious worship of the old order, represented by the Jewish temple, has been found unsatisfactory, what kind of worship is to be offered in the new temple foreshadowed in 2$^{19-21}$? The first approaches to an answer to these questions are given in 3^1 to 4^{26}.

In 3$^{1-21}$, to a friendly representative of the old order at its best, the Lord reveals two truths: first, that the opening of heaven to earth, promised in 1^{51}, which we may paraphrase as the full revelation of God to man, is not due to any activity or effort on man's part, but solely to the descent therefrom of One who alone is able to bridge the gulf between them (3$^{6.13}$*); and secondly, that only he who is reborn from above, by means of water and spirit, can understand these things and see or enter into the kingdom of God, which is or gives eternal life. And in

---

* 'That which is born of the flesh is flesh; and that which is born of the Spirit is spirit.' 'No man hath ascended into heaven, but he that descended out of heaven, even the Son of man.'

3^{16-21} we are once more reminded of the negative side of the matter, if we may so term it; to those who 'love the darkness' and do not 'do the truth' the new order speaks, not of salvation, but of condemnation.

In 3^{22-36} much the same teaching is given (cf., for example, $3^{31\,f.}$ with $3^{6.11.13}$), but now in respect of the contrast between John's work and that of the Lord, and of the supersession of the former by the latter. It need not delay us, and we can pass to 4^{1-26}.·

The conversation of the Lord with the Samaritan woman deals with a twofold contrast, first, that of water, and then that of worship. As regards the first, we recall that in 2^{1-10} water, designed for Jewish methods of purifying, was replaced, at the Lord's bidding, by wine; that in 3^{3-5} a new or heavenly birth, defined as birth by means of water and spirit, is required for the vision of or entrance into the kingdom of God (cf. 1^{51}); and that in 3^{22-36} as the result of a discussion about purifying—again a reference to water—John emphasizes the complete supersession of his work by that of his successor. In 4^{1-15} we now learn that water drawn from Jacob's well cannot be compared with the living or springing water offered by the Lord. As regards the second contrast, that of worship, we recall that in 2^{13-20} the Lord condemned the abuse of worship in the temple at Jerusalem, and implies its coming destruction. In 4^{20-6} we learn that the hour of a true worship of God, with its centre neither in Jerusalem nor in Samaria, is at hand; for the Father, who has sent His Son into the world (3^{17}), is seeking true worshippers; and their true and spiritual worship, it is hinted in the last two verses of the conversation, will be centred on the person of the Lord.

It has been necessary to trace in outline the arrangement and teaching of the first few chapters of this gospel, in order to show that the section 2^{13-22} which deals with the Lord's action in the temple is closely connected with the narratives on each side of it, and can only be understood in relation to them, and indeed to this gospel as a whole; and to this section we now return.

III

In the last book of the Old Testament it is promised that, after a forerunner has been sent to prepare the way, the Lord

Himself will suddenly come to His temple and that, although His coming will be such that none can stand before it, He will purge the sons of Levi, who will then offer to the Lord a righteous offering. The coming and witness of the forerunner, in the person of John, has already been described in this gospel, and in chapter 4 the Samaritan woman will learn that the hour of true worship, that is, of the righteous offering, has arrived; and between these sections we find the fulfilment of the third and chief item of the prophecy, namely, the coming of the Lord to His temple. In accordance, however, with the thought and scheme of this gospel as a whole, in which all Jewish privilege is abolished* and the Jews, like Judas, are 'cast out' (15⁶), by the coming of Christ the Levitical worship, which has been profaned, is destroyed, not cleansed; and its place is taken by a different worship, the nature of which it is one purpose of the later chapters of this gospel to make clear. In this respect, therefore, the fulfilment of the prophecy takes a new and unexpected form, as is shown in the closing verses of the section, 2¹⁹⁻²².

Very strong evidence can be offered to show that the thought of the Lord as the true Passover or Paschal Lamb is constantly present to the mind of the evangelist, from 1²⁹ throughout the book, and is indeed a leading *motif* in his record of the Passion; and his emphasis in 2¹⁴⁻¹⁶ on the expulsion from the temple of all the merchants engaged in traffic in the sacrificial animals, and of the animals themselves, may be due to the same consideration. St. John seldom forces on his readers an interpretation of a story which he records; an interpretation is there, for him who is so minded; but it is left to the reader to discern. Accordingly St. John's teaching here may be that the Jewish temple is now ceasing to be the central seat of the worship of God, and that animal sacrifice will be needed no more.

St. Paul soon found, in his evangelistic work, that as a proof of divine authority the Jews craved for miracle; 'the Jews ask for *sēmeia*' (1 Cor. 1²²). In St. John's gospel part of the implication of the word *sēmeion* is that of a significant action, i.e. an action the meaning or purpose of which must be sought, as it were, below the surface; and it is typical here of his constant irony that, although a *sēmeion* in this sense has just been carried

---

* Consider, for example, the treatment of the Jewish sabbath in 5¹⁶ ᶠ· or that of descent from Abraham in 8³⁵⁻⁵⁹.

out before the eyes of the Jews, if our interpretation of 2¹⁴⁻¹⁶ is correct, they fail to perceive its import, and ask for that which has just been granted. In reply the Lord, in ambiguous language, offers the supreme *sēmeion* of the Gospel, that is, His resurrection; though the Jews may destroy the shrine of the incarnate Word, in a brief period he will raise it (cf. 10¹⁷ᶠ·*). The Jews, as we should expect in this gospel, understand the Lord to refer to the building of stone, and express incredulity; and therewith the conversation, and the description of the incident, are brought abruptly to a close. Only to the reader is the true meaning of the Lord's words revealed (2²¹), with a further note that the Lord's actual resurrection brought the saying itself to the disciples' remembrance and gave them a true understanding both of Old Testament prophecy and of the Lord's words here.

No doubt the reference in 'the shrine of his body' is primarily to the body which was laid in a tomb and raised within three days. But St. John's note that the temple or shrine of the Lord's body was to replace the Jewish temple is likely to have had a further and very significant meaning to his readers. For the idea of the community of believers as a shrine of God (1 Cor. 3¹⁶) or a holy shrine (Eph. 2²¹) which is the body of Christ (1 Cor. 12²⁷) is found in several New Testament epistles, and it will be noticed that these epistles are associated closely with Ephesus, with which place St. John's gospel also is generally believed to be connected. It is true that St. John does not, like St. Paul, use the expression 'the body of Christ' in reference to disciples; but the union of the glorified Lord with His followers is a cardinal doctrine of this gospel; indeed, this union is compared (17²² ᶠ·†) to nothing less than the archetypal union of the Father and the Son. Readers of this gospel therefore would understand further that the temple which the Lord will raise up as a result of His death and resurrection is His mystical body, the Church (Eph. 1²² ᶠ·), in which God is worshipped in spirit (Eph. 2²²) and in truth (Eph. 4¹⁵; cf. John 4²⁴). This worship, however, is only possible if those who offer it are united with their Lord in His ministry, death, and resurrection (cf. Col. 3³‡);

* 'I lay down my life, that I may take it again. . . . I have power to lay it down, and I have power to take it again.'

† 'That they may be one, even as we are one; I in them, and thou in me, that they may be perfected into one.'

‡ 'Ye died, and your life is hid with Christ in God.'

and St. John by his citation in 2^{17} of words from Psalm 69, which is quoted in all the gospels and in other New Testament books in reference to the Passion, has already brought this incident of the cleansing of the temple into connexion with the death of the Lord. There is thus in this story, as elsewhere in St. John's gospel, a triple depth of meaning. First, the Lord performs an act by which He condemns the methods of the existing temple worship. Secondly, this act, as understood by the evangelist, symbolizes the destruction of the old order of worship, that of the Jewish Church, and its replacement by a new order of worship, that of the Christian Church, the shrine of the living God. And thirdly, intermediate between the old order and the new order is the ministry, death, and resurrection of Jesus Christ, which alone makes possible the foundation and the life of the new temple.

IV

If this explanation of St. John's narrative is on the whole correct, and if we remind ourselves that throughout his gospel he seems to handle his historical material with considerable freedom in the interests of theological truth, the position of the story in his record becomes intelligible. For first, in accordance with the prophecy of Malachi, the Lord's coming to the temple is brought into close connexion with the work of the forerunner; and secondly, the negative aspect of the Lord's ministry, which will loom very large in chapters 7 to 9, is combined from the outset, as in the introduction itself (1$^{10-13}$), with the positive aspect, as illustrated in the immediately preceding sign at Cana. Whether in fact the incident took place early or late in the ministry, it is not possible to say with certainty, since the other evangelists, in whose gospels, unlike that of St. John, the Lord only comes to Jerusalem once, and at the end, naturally place it late. If we have to make a choice, we shall probably be right to give the preference to the synoptic rather than to the Johannine setting of the incident; it is an act unparalleled in all that we know of the Lord's life, and likely to have occurred towards the climax of events. It must also have produced extreme tension and excitement; and this condition of affairs is expressed much more clearly by St. Mark, whom St. Matthew and St. Luke follow in the setting of the incident, than by St. John.

Thus the statement in Mark that the Lord allowed no one to carry a vessel through the temple may imply that His supporters seized and guarded the entrances and exits of the temple. It is, however, at any rate possible to show that St. John, whether correct in his chronology or not, is in many respects at one with St. Mark in his understanding of the incident and of its meaning.

For in Mark the cleansing, which takes place on the day after the Lord's entry into the capital, is brought into closest connexion both with the rejection of Israel and with the Lord's own coming death. Thus in Mark the incident is placed between the two sections dealing with the withering of the fig-tree, which, the Lord finds, had indeed the appearance of abundant life but no actual fruit; and it will be remembered that the Lord had entered the temple on the preceding day and had scrutinized it carefully (Mark 11¹¹). Secondly, in the same context there seems to be a reference to the displacement of the mountain of the Lord's house (Mic. 4¹*); but, so far from the realization of the prophecy that it will be exalted above the hills, faith sees that it will be sunk in the depth of the sea (Mark 11²³). Thirdly, on the day after the cleansing, when challenged by the religious leaders and asked to name the authority for His action, the Lord Himself brings the preparatory work of John into connexion with the cleansing. An understanding of the authority by which John had acted would give an understanding of the Lord's authority in the present issue. (And we saw that in the fourth gospel the cleansing of the temple follows very closely upon the work and witness of John.) In Mark this reference to John is immediately followed by the allegory about the behaviour of the tenants of the vineyard, who in the end not only kill the owner's only son, but thereby bring complete loss and ruin on themselves; and here we are not left to conjecture, for the evangelist explicitly adds that the significance and import of the allegory were not lost upon the hearers (Mark 12¹²). Fourthly, a little later, it may be on the same day, for all that St. Mark tells us to the contrary, the Lord predicts the utter destruction of the Jewish temple (Mark 13¹ᶠ·†). And finally,

* 'The mountain of the Lord's house shall be established in the top of the mountains, and it shall be exalted above the hills.'

† 'There shall not be left here one stone upon another, which shall not be thrown down.'

in the course of the examination of the Lord by the Sanhedrin, when the chain of events, set in motion, according to St. Mark, by the cleansing of the temple, has run its course and He is found worthy of death, reference is made (Mark 14^{58}) to a prediction by Him that He would destroy the material Jewish shrine and replace it almost immediately by another shrine, not made with hands.*

Readers of St. Mark's gospel, drawn from all the nations (Mark 11^{17}), were not likely to forget that a prophecy by the Lord of a transformation of worship, to which they owed their life as members of His body, had been one of the factors in His condemnation.†

* Julius Wellhausen, *Einleitung in die drei ersten Evangelien²*, 98, in a reference to the importance of the Lord's words in Mark $13^{1\,f.}$ and their probable connexion with the charge brought against Him in Mark 14^{58}, concludes with the following significant sentence: 'If the Temple of God is destroyed, then all the more the Jewish commonwealth.' The words illustrate strikingly the immense significance to the Jews of their temple.

† I desire to express my obligations, in the preparation of this article, to a study of this passage by Sir Edwyn Hoskyns in *Theology*, September 1920, and to lectures (at present unpublished) by Professor C. H. Dodd on St. John's gospel.

VII

ST. MARK'S GOSPEL—
COMPLETE OR INCOMPLETE?

THE problem of the conclusion of St. Mark's gospel is remarkable enough, even if regard is paid only to the textual phenomena. Westcott and Hort, justifying the exceptionally full treatment which they give to it in their 'Notes on Select Readings',* remark that 'the variation . . . is almost unrivalled in interest and importance, and no other that approaches it in interest and importance stands any longer in need of full discussion'. But the problem, I believe, also deserves study on the religious side; and it is chiefly to this aspect of it that I invite attention. At the moment therefore I will only recall the general agreement at the present time, on the part at any rate of those who regard our second gospel as the earliest of the synoptists, that when copies of it came into the hands of the first and third evangelists it ended at 16⁸. 16⁸ therefore is the oldest ending of the book that we can trace.

It seems therefore that we have to choose one of three possibilities:

1. The author had intended to proceed farther, but was prevented from doing so, whether by death or for some other reason.
2. The author did proceed farther, but at a very early date all that he wrote after 16⁸ was lost.
3. The author ended his work, intentionally, at 16⁸.

The discovery, or recognition, that 16⁸ is the oldest ending which we can reach led to the discussion whether the evangelist can possibly have intended to finish his work, as it was said, so sadly and abruptly; and since in most quarters such an intention was regarded as incredible, the third possibility has thus far received, at any rate in this country, comparatively little attention. Interest was directed rather to the question how the book must or should have ended, and how the loss, if there

---

* *The New Testament in the Original Greek*, vol. 2, 'Notes on Select Readings', 28.

was a loss, occurred. But it is important to keep steadily in mind that, except for the objection just mentioned, the alleged sadness and abruptness of the present ending, there is no evidence of any kind whatever on behalf of either of the first two possibilities;* and the difficulties which they both involve are so great, as is also generally admitted, that it is undesirable to believe the text, as we have it, to be incomplete, 'unless we are compelled to this by the document itself'.†

This then is the real problem, and according to the last sentence it is to be solved, if it can be solved, by reference to the book itself; we are to take account of the outlook, method, and purpose of the author; the evangelist is to be explained, so far as may be, by himself; and we ask therefore, Does a careful consideration of the contents of the document give us any reason to think that the text, as we have it, need not after all be incomplete? But before trying to deal with this question, I desire to draw attention to the opinions, about the ending of Mark, of the veteran scholar Dr. George Salmon, Provost of Trinity College, Dublin, whose *Historical Introduction to the New Testament* deservedly passed through nine editions in the latter years of the nineteenth century. I do not recall his views here from any desire that we should accept his solution of the problem. For Dr. Salmon, writing in the last century, that is, before the considerable advance made in the recent discussion

* Thus there is no suggestion in any extant writing of the apostolic or sub-apostolic age that the ending at 16[8] was regarded as a problem or a difficulty, except for the later addition of the alternative endings. We know nothing for certain about the time when these were added, except that the longer may have been added before A.D. 140 and must have been added considerably before A.D. 188. The evidence is that St. Justin Martyr, about A.D. 140, quotes four words which he may have taken from 16[20]; but, even if this is so, it should be remembered that he may have known the fragment 16[9-20] before it became attached to St. Mark's gospel, since 16[9-20], although now a part of the canonical scriptures, is generally agreed to be the last part of an independent work, the rest of which has perished. It should be added, however, that Tatian's *Diatessaron* may very possibly have included the longer ending; and Tatian had been a pupil of Justin. In any case, St. Irenaeus in A.D. 188 quotes 16[19] as belonging to the end of St. Mark's gospel.

No mention or trace of the shorter ending has been found in any Greek or Latin patristic writing, unless there is an echo of its language in Eusebius' *Ecclesiastical History* 2[14 ad fin.] The textual evidence suggests that it was added in certain quarters not later than at some time in the second century.

† These last words are quoted from an article on this subject by Dr. W. L. Knox in the *Harvard Theological Review*, January 1942, pp. 13 ff. He proceeds to argue that the abrupt ending compels us to regard the work as incomplete. I have ventured to apply his words in a different way.

of the problem, strains every nerve and exercises the utmost ingenuity to persuade us that Mark 16⁹⁻²⁰ was, from the first, part of the book and that there is no compelling reason why the verses should not be ascribed to the writer of the rest of the book, in other words, to St. Mark himself. But in this matter the verdict of the last fifty years has gone decisively and, I believe, unanimously against him. Indeed as early as 1898 we find Dr. Swete writing thus,* 'Unless we entirely misjudge the writer of the second gospel, the last twelve verses [i.e. 16⁹⁻²⁰] are the work of another mind, trained in another school'. We may thus regard it as now agreed that Mark 16⁹⁻²⁰ formed no part of the original gospel according to St. Mark.

My reason for calling attention to Dr. Salmon's opinion on this point is that, holding the views which he did, he is not shut up to or bound to favour *any* of the three possibilities, one of which we now and probably rightly believe must contain the answer to the problem. He is therefore able to estimate and assess their value quite objectively and without any inclination to *parti pris*, and this, I suggest, makes his opinion at least of great interest. Here are his views on the three possibilities.

1. As regards the possibility of loss, he writes:†

We may fairly dismiss as incredible the supposition that the conclusion which St. Mark originally wrote to his Gospel unaccountably disappeared without leaving a trace behind, and was almost universally replaced by a different conclusion. It has been suggested that the last leaf of the original MS. became detached, and perished; and it is true that the loss of a leaf is an accident liable to happen to a MS. Such a hypothesis explains very well the *partial* circulation of defective copies of a work. Suppose, for instance, that a very old copy of St. Mark's Gospel, wanting the last leaf, was brought, let us say, to Egypt. Transcripts made from that venerable copy would want the concluding verses; or if they were added from some other authority, indications might appear that the addition had been made only after the Gospel had been supposed to terminate. In this way might originate a local circulation of a defective family of MSS. But the *total* loss of the original conclusion could not take place in this way, unless the first copy had been kept till it dropped to pieces with age before anyone made a transcript of it, so that a leaf once lost was lost for ever.

---

* *The Gospel according to St. Mark*, 1st ed., p. cv.
† *Introduction to the New Testament*, 9th ed., 149.

2. As to the suggestion that the evangelist died before bringing his work to a conclusion, he writes, 'Even in the supposed case, that St. Mark, after writing verse 8, had a fit of apoplexy, the disciple who gave his work to the world would surely have added a fitting termination'. I should myself wish to put the matter more strongly and to say, with regard to both the suggestions thus far mentioned, that in respect of all such theories as those of mutilation, whether deliberate or accidental, or the writer's sudden death or martyrdom or imprisonment, the question remains, why did not the local church, in which this gospel appeared, at once either restore the original ending or, if this had not been yet written or was not available, at least provide what could be regarded as a suitable conclusion? Since it is agreed that the copies of Mark used by the two other synoptists ended at 16⁸, it seems clear that no such attempt was made; and yet, so far as we can see, there was nothing to prevent it, for we have ample evidence that for some time no special sanctity attached to the text of the books of the New Testament. Indeed, the treatment of the text of Mark by both St. Matthew and St. Luke would be sufficient witness on this point; and each of these two writers probably believed also that his work would entirely supersede the earlier gospel. Nor can there have existed at this time any scrupulous regard for the original form of St. Mark's gospel, on the ground that it was the inviolable work of a single individual, especially if, as many are disposed to believe, this evangelist produced his book with the authority and for the sake of some particular church.

It is important that we should be prepared, if necessary, to consider each gospel by and for itself alone, dismissing from our minds any reference to or comparison with the contents of the other three. This is difficult; thus in the matter under discussion it is hard not to assume that St. Mark must have pursued the course taken by his successors and have included or intended to include, at the end of his book, the record of one or more manifestations of the risen Lord to His disciples. We ought, however, to consider the problems of this gospel by reference to itself alone, and St. Mark above all has every right to claim this of us, since, at the time when he wrote, the other three gospels, as we have reason to believe, did not yet exist. As we shall see in a moment, neglect of this principle can lead to very surprising error.

3. It would have been sufficient for my immediate purpose to give Dr. Salmon's views on two only of the three possibilities; but perhaps in fairness I ought to quote from him as regards the third possibility, which it is the purpose of this paper to uphold. I do so the less unwillingly, because it will be seen that Dr. Salmon has been led into a remarkable mis-statement, which at once goes far to weaken the value of his opinion about this third possibility.

It has been imagined [he writes] that the Gospel [of St. Mark] never had a formal conclusion [*sic*]; but this also I find myself unable to believe. Long before any gospel was written, the belief in the Resurrection of our Lord had become universal among Christians, and this doctrine had become the main topic of every Christian preacher. A history [*sic*] of our Lord, in which this cardinal point was left unmentioned, may be pronounced inconceivable. And if there were no doctrinal objection, there would be the literary one— that no Greek writer would give his work so abrupt and ill-omened a termination as ἐφοβοῦντο γάρ.

Dr. Salmon implies, it will be noticed, that 'the cardinal point' of the resurrection is 'left unmentioned' in Mark 16^{1-8}. And if it be thought that blindness, due no doubt to the un-conscious influence of the unjustified presuppositions just mentioned, could hardly further go, I feel bound to quote an equally remarkable sentence from Dr. Hort* which errs—and again, may we not say, for the same reason—in precisely the opposite direction. He is arguing that St. Mark's gospel cannot have been designed to end at 16^8. 'When it is seen', he says, 'how Matthew 28^{1-7} is completed by Matthew 28^{8-10}, and Luke 24^{1-7} by Luke $24^{8,9}$, it becomes incredible not merely that St. Mark should have closed a paragraph with a γάρ, but that his one detailed account of an appearance of the Lord on the morning of the resurrec-tion should end upon a note of unassuaged terror.' As against Dr. Salmon, the message of the resurrection is indeed the cardinal content of Mark 16^{1-8}, especially verse 6. On the other hand, as against Dr. Hort, there is in these verses no record of an appearance, detailed or otherwise, of the risen Lord. It seems clear that the presuppositions of these two great men, owing to their comparison of Mark 16^{1-8} with the contents of the other gospels, alone explain how and why they came to

* Op. cit., 47.

make these remarkable slips.* The errors illustrate very well how difficult it was, even for two of the leading teachers of the last century, to escape from preconceptions in a matter of this kind, and are a warning to us to do our utmost to rid ourselves of the same tendency.

But before we leave Dr. Salmon, let me emphasize once more my chief purpose in drawing attention to his views. My contention, it will be remembered, is that he had no axe to grind in this matter, since he believed Mark 16⁹⁻²⁰ to be the original ending of the gospel, and that therefore his opinion as regards both the theories widely held in this country to-day is of value. And his opinion was, that both the theories are impossible.

Let us now consider the objections raised to the view which sees the deliberate conclusion of the book at Mark 16⁸. These objections may be summarized under four heads:†

1. The sentence, still more the paragraph, and, most of all, the book cannot end with the word γάρ; the suggestion is intolerable.

2. The word ἐφοβοῦντο, on the literary side, requires a conclusion: either a direct object, or a completing infinitive, or a μή clause.

3. The word ἐφοβοῦντο also causes difficulty on the psychological side, a difficulty indeed which extends to the whole of verse 8. We must be shown that the women's fear was dispelled, and their silence and disobedience resolved.

4. One or more manifestations of the risen Lord must be narrated, and the more so, because 14²⁸ and 16⁷ point the way to them; and the book must end on the notes of victory and happiness.

Let us consider these objections in turn.

First, the philological difficulty as regards γάρ. It will no doubt be agreed that St. Mark shows a strong tendency to form short sentences with γάρ; more than twenty cases could be cited. Some of the most striking are 1¹⁶ ἦσαν γάρ ἁλιεῖς, 5⁴² ἦν γάρ ἐτῶν

Δώδεκα, 9⁶ ἔκφοβοι γὰρ ἐγένοντο, 11¹⁸ ἐφοβοῦντο γὰρ αὐτόν, 16⁴ ἦν γὰρ μέγας σφόδρα. I have also elsewhere* drawn attention to two striking examples of similar usage in the LXX translation of Genesis: 18¹⁵ And Sarah denied, saying, I laughed not, ἐφοβήθη γάρ, and 45³ And Joseph said to his brethren, I am Joseph; doth my father yet live? And his brethren could not answer him, ἐταράχθησαν γάρ. And finally a reference to *c.* 32 of Justin Martyr's *Dialogue with Trypho the Jew* is of especial interest, since there the words ἐσταυρώθη γάρ end a paragraph, though they form part, it is true, of a conversation, not of a narrative. It must be admitted frankly that, if the words ἐφοβοῦντο γάρ end both the narrative paragraph here and the book itself, no exact parallel can be found, either in Mark, so far as the end of a paragraph narrative is concerned, or elsewhere in Greek literature, though it is said that some further light on the matter will be forthcoming in the fourth edition of Bauer's *Wörterbuch*. I am not myself sufficiently well versed in the literary usages of this period to be entitled to an opinion on the point; but I am impressed by the very little difficulty which classical scholars, whether in print or in conversation, seem to find in it.†

It will, however, be necessary to say more, in connexion with the second objection, on the possibility that the words ἐφοβοῦντο γάρ conclude the gospel, and at present I content myself by drawing attention to St. Mark's general usage of γάρ.

The second objection, raised on literary grounds, is that ἐφοβοῦντο is unlikely to be used absolutely; it needs a completing accusative or an infinitive or a μή clause. This objection seems to me the weakest of the four, since the matter is decisively settled by Marcan usage. Apart from 16⁸, φοβεῖσθαι occurs ten times in this gospel: four times with a personal object, individual or collective; once with an explanatory accusative, φόβον μέγαν; once with an infinitive; and four times absolutely; it is never followed in Mark by a μή clause. Above all, I wish to draw attention to 10³², οἱ δὲ ἀκολουθοῦντες ἐφοβοῦντο. If no one, as I believe is the case, has seen any difficulty in this absolute use

---

* *Locality and Doctrine in the Gospels*, pp. 10 ff., where further examples from other literature are given. Cf. also Cicero, *Ad Atticum* xii. 12. 2, Ad antiquos igitur; ἀνεμέσητον γάρ. Cicero then passes to the concluding sentences of his letter.

† Thus Professor Ulrich von Wilamowitz-Moellendorff, who regards 16⁸ as the deliberate conclusion of the book, sees no difficulty at all here, on the literary side: *Reden und Vorträge* (2 Band, 4 Auflage, 1926).

of the verb at 10^{32}, why should the same word cause difficulty at 16^8?

It will be convenient to begin our consideration of the third objection, the difficulty raised by 16^8 on the psychological side, with an attempt to answer the question which has just been put. For it seems likely that the real reason, why objection is raised to the absolute use of ἐφοβοῦντο in 16^8, lies in the sentence as a whole, 'They said nothing to anyone, for they were afraid'. What is desired is really an explanation of the *silence*, and therefore the objection is raised that ἐφοβοῦντο requires further definition; for the silence is said to be due to fear; of what then were the women afraid? To this objection two answers may be made, each, as it seems to me, satisfactory in its own sphere. First, St. Mark elsewhere uses verbs of emotion without direct or precise explanation. I have already referred to 10^{32}, and I could also appeal to that *crux interpretum* 9^{15}; why do we read, after the Lord's descent from the mount of Transfiguration, that all the multitude, when it saw him, ἐξεθαμβήθη? St. Mark does not explain, any more than he explains his use of the same verb at 16^6, in the passage which we are now considering. But, secondly, the context itself does indeed contain an all-sufficient explanation of the women's fear in 16^8. For in the first part of this verse we have already been told that they were seized with trembling and astonishment, and it is clear that these emotions were caused by their experience on their entry into (or, it may be, with a different reading, their arrival at) the tomb. Is it not most unlikely and indeed unreasonable to suppose that the cause of their fear at the end of verse 8 is different from the cause of their trembling and astonishment at the beginning of the verse? Their silence, like that of Ezekiel, 3^{26} 24^{27}, or of Zacharias, the father of the Baptist, after he has received the vision and message of Gabriel, Luke 1^{20}, or of St. Paul in 2 Corinthians 12^{4*}, is due to their experience. They have received a command, but owing to the unnerving effect which it has had upon them they are unable to obey it.

Several of the attempts to reconstruct the assumed lost ending suggest that this interpretation of the demand for an explicit explanation of the women's fear is correct. For in these

---

* Is not the natural translation here, 'he . . . heard unspeakable words, which it is not possible for a man to utter'?

reconstructions the women's silence is regarded as due to fear of men, whether fear of the Jews or of the disciples' reaction to their message, if they gave it; in other words, it is a reflective, calculating fear; whereas I desire to submit that the whole tenor of 16^{1-8} shows the amazement, flight, trembling, astonishment, and finally fear on the part of the women to have been due to fear or dread of God, to fear caused by revelation, and not to fear of men.

And happily we are not left here to conjecture; if it be granted that we are right to try to explain St. Mark by St. Mark, we are able to control his procedure, and to say with confidence what kind of fear he has in mind. In the whole of his book there is perhaps no section which in form presents closer parallels to the section which we are now considering than the section of the stilling of the storm, 4^{35-41}. The central feature of that story is the Lord's rebuke to the elements, whereupon we read that the wind ceased and there ensued a great calm. The disciples' earlier anxiety was therefore no longer necessary or natural, and they should have been forthwith at peace; but on the contrary their earlier physical alarm is now replaced by a much deeper fear. For the story then proceeds with the Lord's rebuke to the disciples, 'Why are ye cowardly? have ye not yet (or, ye have not yet) faith?', words which may be compared with the words addressed to the women at 16^5, 'Be not amazed'; and finally we read, 'And they were afraid with a great fear, and began to say one to another, Who then is this, that even the wind and the sea obey him?' Is it not clear that the silence of the women at 16^8 and the inarticulate, bewildered utterance of the disciples at 4^{41} are not very different and that they arise from the same cause, namely, an increasing and involuntary realization of the nature and being of Him with whom they have to do. And if this is so, then suddenly to come back, in the last words of 16^8, to the thought of the fear of men would be a most painful and indeed intolerable anti-climax, and utterly unworthy of St. Mark.

It is true that St. Mark does not elsewhere explicitly refer to silence as the result of fear of God, or, in other words, of revelation. We have just seen that in 4^{35-41} the disciples' dread ends in an utterance, although I suggest that according to Marcan usage the words at 9^{32}, after the second proclamation of the Passion, 'But they understood not the saying, and were afraid to ask him', would have been, except for one point to be considered later, an equally satisfactory conclusion to the story of the stilling of the storm. A reason, however, may be suggested why the combination of fear and silence is reserved for the last sentence of the book and occurs there only. It has often been noticed that St. Mark does not describe but only indicates the resurrection. The reserve with which he treats the subject may be compared with the reserve with which he describes its counterpart, the crucifixion; and here I rejoice to be able to quote some words of Professor Dodd. In speaking of the Passion in Mark he says,* 'The dramatic movement of events is indeed rendered with a vigorous and convincing realism; but from time to time St. Mark drops unobtrusive hints of an inner drama which supplies the deeper meaning of the events. The reader whose imagination is awake is made to feel that he is looking into great depths.'† And just as nothing can exceed the unspeakable tragedy and darkness of the Passion, as recorded by St. Mark, so nothing, I suggest, can exceed, in his view, the ineffable wonder and mystery of its parallel or counterpart, the resurrection. The one unique event is answered by the other; and it is therefore possible that in 16$^{1-8}$ an emphasis, unsurpassed elsewhere, even in this gospel, is laid upon the devastating results, for the women, of the first intimations of the greatest and final manifestation of the divine activity recorded in this book.

We have still to deal with that part of the third objection which requires from the evangelist an explicit statement that the women's fears were dispelled and their silence and disobedience overcome. But before we try to show that verse 8, without further addition, is a possible conclusion to the passage, let us first consider 16$^{1-8}$ as a single section. It has indeed been urged that a perfect Marcan section, in respect of chronology and otherwise, must be completely independent of its context on either side, and must contain within itself all that is necessary for the understanding of it, like the stories of the cleansing of

---

* In a broadcast to schools, 31 May 1948.

† This view seems to me clearly much nearer to the truth than that of Dr. W. L. Knox, who in the article already mentioned, arguing that 16^8 cannot have been intended to be the conclusion, says with reference not only to 16$^{1-8}$ but to the book as a whole, 'In no case are the actions or words as recorded intended to leave anything to our imagination'.

the leper 1⁴⁰⁻⁴⁵ or that of the anointing of the Lord 14³⁻⁹;
whereas 16¹⁻⁸ is an essential part of the story of the Passion; it
begins with a precise note of time and is linked directly with the
preceding narrative. To these phenomena, however, have we
not an exact parallel in Mark 1²⁹⁻³¹, a passage where we are
possibly, perhaps probably, in direct contact with Petrine
reminiscence?* This section is usually regarded as an altogether
satisfactory Marcan unit, containing all the essential parts of a
'pericope'. But, if so, we are entitled to notice that it begins
with a precise note of time, linking it with the preceding section,
a feature which, as we have already seen, is found also in 16¹⁻⁸,
and that some of the persons mentioned have appeared in the
preceding narrative, a point which is true also of one at any rate
of those mentioned in 16¹⁻⁸.

If then we may approach 16¹⁻⁸ as a single section, although
it begins with a definite note of time and is also linked in other
ways with the preceding record of the Passion, we may analyse
it thus. The introduction states the situation; the conversation
of the women prepares the way for the coming disclosure and
also heightens the sense of expectation. We then pass to the
central feature of the story, the angelic presence and message;†
and finally we are told of the impression which these produce
upon the women. In connexion with this final trait, we notice
that the following words are used in this section of the women's
mental state: ἐκθαμβεῖσθαι (twice), τρόμος, ἔκστασις, φοβεῖσθαι;
and as regards their action, that they quit the tomb in flight.
Let us now consider these facts in the light of the rest of this
book, in which a frequent result of divine revelation is fear,
whether on the part of disciples or of bystanders, and also
amazement and astonishment. As examples of fear we may cite
the section, already mentioned, on the stilling of the storm;
the section of the Gerasene demoniac; and the fear of the three
disciples at the Transfiguration. As examples of astonishment
we have the initial section on the expulsion of the demoniac
in the Capernaum synagogue; the section of the healing of the
palsied man; that of the restoration of the daughter of the ruler

---

* See p. 21.

† I think it is not open to doubt that we are meant to discern an angelic being
in the young man of verse 6; cf. 2 Macc. 3²⁶·³³; and both the first and third
evangelists thus understand the term. For the significance of white garments in this
connexion cf. Mark 9³, Acts 1¹⁰.

of the synagogue; the section 6⁴⁵⁻⁵², in which the wind ceases when
the Lord rejoins the disciples in the boat on the lake; and that
of the healing of the deaf man who also had difficulty in speaking.
But here two points call for notice.

First, although according to St. Mark the first and inevitable
result of the realization by men of the presence of revelation is
fear or astonishment or both together, such fear or astonishment
is not by any means the purpose of the revelation, and in itself
is undesirable; it is indeed solely due to human lack of understanding or of insight.* More than once in this book the Lord
deprecates its hold on men, attributing its power over them to
their want of faith and, in the case of disciples, to want of
understanding of their Master.† Similarly in Mark 6¹⁻⁶, the
section of the Lord's rejection in his *patris*, the neighbours who
are astonished in verse 2 are caused to stumble in him in verse 3;
and in verse 6 their ἀπιστία, their lack of faith, is said to be the
cause of their offence.

The second point which calls for notice is connected with the
structure of this gospel. It has often been noticed that demon-
strations of the Lord's messianic power are frequent before the
Caesarea Philippi section but, after that, comparatively rare. And
in this first half of the book fear and astonishment are caused more
by these messianic acts, than by the teaching given. The Caesarea
Philippi section, however, contains the confession by St. Peter,
on behalf of the disciples, of the Lord's Messiahship. In F. C.
Burkitt's striking words,‡ 'St. Peter, being now aware of the
Messiahship of Jesus, is thereby put on the same footing as the
demons'—who hitherto alone have shown this knowledge.

If therefore fear and astonishment are the result of unbelief,
we are justified in expecting that, when acts of messianic power
occur *after* Caesarea Philippi, they will no longer cause these
reactions in the disciples; and this is in fact the case.‖ On the
other hand, as is made vividly clear in the Caesarea Philippi
section itself, St. Peter's confession is at present very far from

---

* *'Primus in orbe deos fecit timor* (Statius, *Theb.* 3⁶⁶¹); but when we know what He is
whom our fears first imagined, we discover that He is love. . . . Perfect love casts
out fear (1 John 4¹⁸), but the fear must be there; it is, as we know, the beginning of
wisdom (Ps. 111¹⁰)', C. C. J. Webb, 'The notion of Revelation', in *Pan-Anglican
Papers*, S.P.C.K., 1908.   † See especially 6⁵⁰⁻², 8²¹.
‡ *The American Journal of Theology*, xv. 2 (April 1911), p. 189.
‖ I am indebted at this point to a valuable paper by the Rev. J. C. Fenton, M.A.

including knowledge of the true meaning and implications of the Messiahship of the Lord, who is to be a suffering Messiah and whose disciples are to suffer with Him; and from this point to the end of the book the emphasis lies on this new teaching rather than on the acts of power; and it is *this teaching* which now causes amazement or astonishment and fear. Further, because the disciples cannot understand the doctrine of the cross, on the mount of Transfiguration the three cannot understand the doctrine of the Crown, if we may so call it, as there revealed; Peter 'knew not what to answer; for they became sore afraid'. Is it not possible, then, that the reaction of the women at the tomb, their amazement, trembling, astonishment, and fear, gathers up the emotions caused, throughout the book, first by the Lord's messianic actions and secondly by his teaching on the meaning of those messianic actions? In 16$^{1-8}$ the women are faced by His action in the resurrection, and also by the divine teaching in verses 6 and 7; and owing to their imperfect faith, their lack of insight or understanding, call it what you will, the result is inevitable, and their behaviour and reaction are in full accord with all that St. Mark has already taught us in these matters.

For this reason I distrust any suggestion that St. Mark's mention of the silence of the women has some exceptional or ulterior motive, the suggestion for example that he desires to explain why the story of 16$^{1-8}$ did not become known at once within the early Church. It is a characteristic of the little gospel sections, of which, as we have seen, 16$^{1-8}$ is an excellent example, to give a picture of a single situation, with a concentration of interest on some central point. In this section the centre of interest is in the scene which confronts the women at (or it may be, in) the tomb, and in the divine teaching which explains it; everything else is secondary to this central feature, and is the result of it. The questions therefore should not be raised, whether the women conquered their fear, or how long they remained silent; such questions are not in the mind of the evangelist; and in the last verse he is only concerned to emphasize human inadequacy, lack of understanding, and weakness in the presence of supreme, divine action and its meaning. It has been remarked, that 'St. Mark's gospel offers small comfort or support to believers in natural wisdom or virtue'.*

* A. M. Farrer, *The Glass of Vision*, p. 143.

We pass to the fourth and last objection: the book must have ended or been meant to end with one or more manifestations of the risen Lord Himself, and the more so, since the Lord's words in 14²⁸, repeated at 16⁷ in the angelic message, expressly point the way towards this. St. Mark's gospel follows closely the pattern of the *kerygma*, which, it is alleged, always included such a mention; the evangelist therefore could not have intentionally omitted it. And the book must end on the notes of victory and happiness.

Clearly it is regarded as a kind of canon that a gospel must end with a narrative of one or more manifestations of the risen Lord. Let us then put this canon to the test. First, is it unfair to point out that such a canon is applicable only to the first and fourth gospels? If St. Luke's gospel or the first chapter of Acts be regarded as the standard, not only the second gospel but the first and fourth must also be regarded as inadequate and incomplete, for they mention no final outward parting of the Lord from His disciples for the heavenly session. If we also take into consideration the apocryphal gospels, we see how strong the tendency became, to extend the tradition at the end as well as at the beginning of His earthly life. Is it not possible that everything except the fact of the resurrection may be regarded as an appendix to the story of the Lord? And to the fact of the resurrection St. Mark has given full expression in 16¹⁻⁸—a point which, as we have seen, is sometimes overlooked. And this is not all; for, in the second place, our documents reveal an increasing tendency to present the risen Lord as returning to the conditions of earthly life*, whereas the oldest form of the tradition, as Professor Dodd has been at pains to teach us, seems, like the later Creeds themselves, to have connected His resurrection above all, or at once, with His exaltation to the Father's side. In addition to the speeches of St. Peter in the early chapters of Acts, we may quote, in support of this view, such a passage as Romans 8³⁴, 'It is Christ Jesus that died, yea rather, that was raised from the dead, who is at the right hand of God'. If this is correct, a certain lapse of time is required, before a tendency

---

* A study of the gospels of St. Luke and St. John, to which indeed we may add Matt. 28⁹, will suggest that the motive of this tendency was to illustrate and emphasize the identity of Him, who now thus revealed Himself, with the Lord whom the disciples had known in the days of His flesh. Matt. 28¹⁷ᵉⁿᵈ may be understood as suggesting that some had tended to question this identity.

arises to co-ordinate manifestations of the risen Lord with stories of His life and activity, during His ministry. Even St. Matthew's gospel may be cited in favour of this view. For if we may leave out of account the meeting of the Lord with the women in Jerusalem as they return from the tomb, when they receive afresh the instructions which have just been given to them by the angel, the great scene on the mountain-top in Galilee, when the Church receives its marching-orders, is very much more than an appearance-story; rather, the Lord's work on earth having been completed, we have here a manifestation in majesty of the universal Judge. In this connexion I myself am also much impressed with the Marcan form of the three proclamations of the Passion; they all end with a definite but very brief reference to the resurrection. This seems to me to agree closely with the actual achievement of the evangelist in writing chapters 14^1 to 16^8. And the fact that at Mark 16^8 the whole evangelic agreement ceases at one stroke may perhaps be additional evidence that the oldest gospel tradition did not or did not necessarily include one or more accounts of a manifestation of the risen Lord.

Conceivably also St. Paul's language in 1 Cor. 15^{3-8} may be used to give support to the possibility which I am upholding, although the passage is usually regarded as pointing in the opposite direction. In recalling to his readers what he transmitted to them, St. Paul has four clauses, each beginning with ὅτι, and referring respectively to the Lord's death, burial, resurrection, and appearance to Cephas. Thus far his words may not unnaturally be held to strengthen the theory of an incomplete gospel of St. Mark. But it should be remembered that the last ὅτι, with reference to the appearance to Cephas, covers not only it but five further appearances (not including the final appearance to St. Paul), and that these five are therefore all co-ordinated. In other words, the appearance to Cephas is regarded as the first of a succession; and importance now becomes attached to the persons to whom the manifestations were granted, in strong contrast to the impersonality, as we may put it, of the earlier clauses. It may therefore be permissible to regard the final ὅτι clause, which covers five separate manifestations of the risen Lord (or six, if we include that to St. Paul), with a definite reference, on each occasion, to the recipient or recipients of the manifestation, as connected rather with the nascent life of the Church than with the resurrection. If so, it is not surprising that, when Pentecost came to be regarded as the birthday of the Church, there should be a corresponding tendency to attach stories of appearances of the risen Lord to the story of the resurrection rather than to that of the life of the Church.

We still have to consider a further part of the fourth objection: does not Mark 14^{28}, repeated and amplified in 16^7, expressly promise to the disciples a reunion with their Lord in Galilee; and are not the verses only explicable if their purpose is to prepare the way for something yet to be narrated, which will prove their truth? Such an explanation of the passages is not unnatural, but it is not necessary, and may be found to be only an assumption. For, in the first place, St. Mark assumes throughout that his readers are acquainted with the root-facts of the Christian religion; the way in which the Lord is brought upon the scene in 1^9 would alone be sufficient evidence of this. The evangelist is writing for believers who already knew the facts of the Gospel, and, still more important, had day by day in themselves and in the evidence of the progress of the Gospel the witness of the power which the manifestation of the risen Lord first infused into disciples. And, in the second place, there are other examples in the gospels of a promise, the fulfilment of which is not actually recorded in the books themselves. Thus all four gospels record the assurance of the Baptist that his successor brings a baptism 'in Holy Spirit'; but the fourth alone records the fulfilment of the promise. Again, if the end of St. Luke's gospel had been lost, could not the same argument have been used with regard to Luke 22$^{31.32}$, where the Lord clearly implies that St. Peter's fall will be for the moment only, as is often used with regard to the promise about the reunion in Galilee in Mark 14^{28} and 16^7? Would it not have been said that the closing sections of St. Luke's gospel must at least have included the story of St. Peter's recovery, perhaps also of his reinstatement? But clearly St. Luke did not think so; for it will hardly be contended that the passing reference in Luke 24^{34} meets this need. And the reason why he did not think so may perhaps be that the Lord's word was regarded as sufficient to guarantee the subsequent fact, which it was therefore unnecessary to relate; and further, we may add, the life of the Church itself testified to the fact of the recovery and restoration of St. Peter. Accordingly St. Mark may have been willing to leave the reunion in Galilee unrelated, partly because the divine word at 14^{28} and 16^7 has already guaranteed it, and partly, I suggest very seriously, because the event did not lend itself to narration in a book, any more than the experience of St. Paul in 2 Corinthians 12^4, to which I have already referred. It is a matter of constant surprise to me that the revelation of the risen Lord to His disciples seems often to be treated as if it were barely more than a remarkable event, whereas we have every reason to believe that at first the solid earth must have seemed to reel beneath their feet, and the stars to be about to fall. And, if this be so, 14^{28} and 16^7 perhaps do not necessarily prepare for a story which must be told later, but *represent* the fact which the statement foretells. (See further on this point pp. 106–16.)

It remains only to deal with the objection that St. Mark's gospel cannot have ended, as it has been said, 'so sadly'. In the words of Dr. W. L. Knox,* 'Mark has only just reached what is, after all, the main point of his gospel, and the real "happy ending" on which the whole faith of the Church depended'.

It might be sufficient to reply that, even if verse 8 is sad, no Christian readers of the book would go astray in consequence. As I have remarked already, they were well aware of the root-facts of their Gospel. But I would much prefer to contend that, in the light of 16^{1-8} as a whole, the last verse is not to be regarded as sad, in the sense in which the supposed objector uses the word. For to the instructed reader, from the very beginning of this section, with its passing references to the sabbath, the time of divine rest, being now over, and to the sun, the light of the world, having now risen, everything behind the Marcan reserve cries out of the divine victory and love and triumph; and the view that verse 8 is contrary to this impression is due, I suggest, to an incomplete perception of the Marcan method. For, as we have seen is often elsewhere the case in this book, the description of the reaction of the women throws into very strong relief the supremacy and greatness of the section's central teaching, and that teaching is the fact and the message of the Lord's victory and love. Throughout this book, and to the end, we find human failure and want of understanding; but the

* *Harvard Theological Review*, xxxv. 1, Jan. 1942, p. 22.

divine foundation stands firm, and in this book has its final seal in the fact of the resurrection of the Lord.

I desire to suggest, in conclusion, that it may be exceptionally difficult for the present generation to sympathize with St. Mark's insistence on fear and amazement as the first and inevitable and, up to a point, right result of revelation. One of the most obvious and disturbing phenomena in the religious life of Christendom during the last seventy or eighty years has been the disappearance of the awe or dread or holy fear of God. We of the present older generation are not afraid, as our parents and grandparents always were afraid. It is not a marked feature of religious life to-day that we work out our own salvation with fear and trembling, Philippians 2^{12}, or that we offer service well-pleasing to God with godly fear and awe, Hebrews 12^{28}, or that we order our lives, whilst we live here, in fear, 1 Peter 1^{17}; and I doubt whether to most Europeans to-day the words of Joseph to his brethren, 'This do, and live; for I fear God',* would at once give the natural and obvious reason for his forbearance towards them. And it will scarcely be suggested that this has come about, because we have attained the perfect love which casts out fear. The Christian doctrine of eternal life, which is indissolubly connected with that of the Lord's resurrection, is, in the true sense of the word, a tremendous and, on one side, a terrible truth; if we do not know for ourselves that this is so, we are far astray. And if the belief should ever come to be widely held that St. Mark may have ended his book deliberately at 16^8, I should like to think that such a recognition might have its part to play in recalling men and women to the truth that the dread as well as the love of God is an essential note of our religion, which sounds loudly in the New Testament as well as in the Old, and in no book of the New Testament more strongly than in the Gospel according to St. Mark. And St. Mark's conclusion, stylistically harsh and abrupt though it may seem to us and doubtless is, may be as appropriate for him, as the delivery of 'the marching orders of the Church'† on the mountain in Galilee is for St. Matthew, and the idyll of the life of the first disciples in Jerusalem is for St. Luke.

* Gen. 42^{18}.
† As the Duke of Wellington described Matt. $28^{19 f.}$.

VIII

FORM CRITICISM AND THE STUDY
OF THE GOSPELS

SOME time ago a writer in the *Expository Times* expressed the belief that 'the whole basis of the form-criticism theory' is likely 'to dissolve and vanish in a short time'. I have no wish at all to come forward as a champion of claims put out for form criticism, especially as I find that I am often, though I hope wrongly, believed to be such; but since regret has been publicly expressed, both in America and in Germany, at the slowness of this country to recognize the importance of this recent development in New Testament studies, I will try to show why I do not think that the view quoted above is likely to prove to be correct, and indeed why in my opinion we ought not to hope that it should so prove.

In order to appreciate the new study and its methods, we must go back to the beginning of the present century. At that time 'liberal theology' in gospel studies was in the ascendant, and its exponents were filled with a great hope, that of the discovery, or recovery, of 'plain biography'. As a result of more than one hundred years of minute, critical study of the first three gospels, it was believed that two primary documents had been isolated from the mass of the material; and it was hoped that these two primary documents, Mark and Q, would prove bedrock for the ascertainment of the truth about the Lord. For His life, we were invited to study the simple and historically reliable narrative of St. Mark; while for His teaching we could turn to Q, supplemented by the special source of St. Luke. Harnack's course of sixteen lectures, delivered in the winter of 1899–1900 at Berlin, and translated into English under the title *What is Christianity?*, is the best expression of this phase of gospel study, and of its religious value.

In the very next year, however, the axe was laid at the root of the tree. In a book which raised more questions than it solved, W. Wrede, a professor at Breslau, who died in 1906, showed that even Mark is by no means 'plain biography', but reveals definite dogmatic interest, and contains in certain respects an

already highly developed tradition. Wrede was speedily followed by Julius Wellhausen, whose 'brief and pregnant commentaries' on the synoptic gospels, with an accompanying
volume of Introduction, contain, according to the late Professor
J. M. Creed, writing in 1930, 'the seeds of the more important
developments of recent years'. Both Wrede and Wellhausen
urged that in estimating the contents of the gospels we must
consider also the circumstances and needs of those who first
produced and used them, and that some allowance must be
made for this factor. No doubt, in opening up untrodden paths,
these scholars were guilty of over-emphasis and exaggeration;
but they showed conclusively that the life and experiences of
the Church, in the period before the gospels took their present
form, were not without influence upon the way in which the
traditions were transmitted.

English scholars, however, were not quickly moved from the
earlier method of study of the gospels, of which an outline was
traced above. Professor F. C. Burkitt's *The Gospel History and
its Transmission* (1906) shows no clear sign of the coming change
of interest; and this is true even of Dr. B. H. Streeter's *The Four
Gospels* (1924), which may be regarded as the final and most
complete expression in English of the methods and results of
source criticism.

But indeed the tide had turned long before 1924. There has
been little real advance in the purely literary study of the gospels
since the beginning of this century. Students have occupied
themselves in testing the evidence more surely, in elaborating
the proofs of their hypotheses, and in the effort to come to closer
grips with the special sources of the first and third gospels.
But the results have not been commensurate with the expendi-
ture of labour. For example it is, I believe, correct to say that
the Proto-Luke hypothesis is less widely accepted on the
Continent and in America than in this country. Above all, the
hope which inspired the research of fifty years ago has not been
realized. Too many problems remain.

It is important to emphasize this, since the new study of form
criticism is liable to misrepresentation and caricature, unless it is
seen as the logical issue of that form of gospel study which
immediately preceded it. The work of source criticism, which
has produced results of permanent value, is probably now upon

the whole complete; and, rightly viewed, form criticism is the natural and indeed inevitable development of the earlier study.

What then were the defects or imperfections in the earlier study, that is, the purely literary comparison of the synoptic gospels, the greatest triumph of which was the discovery of the priority of Mark? What were the questions raised by Wrede and Wellhausen, to which it could not give an answer? In a single sentence, literary criticism of the gospels does not by itself take us back far enough. The span of at least a generation separates the earliest literary sources, of which we can be sure, from the life of Jesus Christ. If it is said that there must have been eye-witnesses of the ministry still living at the end of this period and indeed much longer, who will have kept the original tradition unimpaired, i.e. historically accurate, we are bound to notice how certain Marcan stories are altered in the first and third gospels, and to ask whether we are justified in assuming that such alterations in the tradition first began after Mark became well known. Rather, does not the treatment of Mark by the first and third evangelists suggest, either that the book was not regarded as too reliable for any alteration, or perhaps rather that other interests were at work in addition to that of the preservation of an exact historical tradition?

Again, when we consider the immense changes in the life of the Church which took place between, say, A.D. 35 and 65, changes in its constituent elements, its geographical extension, its language, its religious outlook, and when we recall that an oral tradition is naturally fluid, we find that we have to ask many questions, into which it was not necessary for source criticism, fully occupied with the literary comparison of the gospels, to probe. Why did the Church produce gospels, a form of writing peculiar to Christianity, and how do these books differ from a history? Why did this form of writing persist, long after the appearance of the canonical gospels, into an age when the later authors had no new reliable historical material to offer? What can we learn about the form or forms in which the tradition of the Lord's words and deeds was handed down? How far, if at all, have the later experiences of the Church affected the narration of His words and deeds? And last, not least, whatever other interests the gospels were designed to serve, can we trust them also to give us a truly historical impression of the ministry, and of the teaching, of the Lord?

No doubt such questions as these were in the background of men's thoughts long before the present generation; but it is only in the last thirty years that a critical and scientific attempt has been made to answer them; and there is bound to be some discomfort and uncertainty, especially for the older generation, as we adjust ourselves to the new study. The name form criticism is, indeed, unfortunate, since it suggests that the study is concerned only with the analysis of the gospel material into the various forms, in which the tradition is found. This is of course a prominent part of the discipline, and in it some valuable results have been achieved. Thus it is now becoming widely recognized that, with the exception of the Passion narrative, which is likely to have been told from the first as a connected story, the gospels consist, so far as narrative is concerned, for the most part of short stories, and that each such story was originally a separate unit. Even where, in our gospels, a connecting link exists between one story and the next, there is reason to think that in many cases the link may be due to the evangelist. Such topographical or chronological information as these links contain may of course be based on other tradition available to the evangelist and as reliable as that of the stories which the links are used to join; but the links themselves probably did not originally form part of the stories now thus joined together. Karl Ludwig Schmidt, in a book entitled *Der Rahmen der Geschichte Jesu*, gave the first thorough demonstration of this important point. Again, stories originally separate, but having the same or a similar character or lesson, tend to be found joined together into groups; but we must not assume that the order, in which we now find the stories, is that in which the events narrated actually occurred; the motive in the arrangement seems to have been topical, rather than historical; thus we have the five 'conflict-stories' placed together in Mark 2^1 to 3^6, each containing or leading up to a 'Gospel-saying' of the Lord. We can sometimes trace the same methods at work in the arrangement of the sayings; thus in Mark 9^{38-50} one object seems to be to aid the memory by a system of 'link-words'.

But the new study does not confine itself to an analysis of the nature and form of the materials contained in the gospels.

Accepting the single story as the unit, it seeks to relate the several stories to the life of the Church which cherished and preserved them, and made use of them to convey its message to the world; and this promises to be the most valuable aspect of the method. In this way the gospels can be to us not only the source of almost all our knowledge of the ministry of Jesus Christ, but also, within limits which need to be carefully guarded, a mirror of the hopes and aspirations, the problems and the difficulties, of the early Church. The stimulus and interest which have already been aroused by the method are due chiefly to this side of its work, which brings into clearer light than ever before the purely *religious* purpose of the gospels. It also shows us why the Church, engrossed in its worship, its teaching and evangelistic work, its controversies and its hopes, was on the whole so little concerned, when handing on traditions of its Master's life, with details of time or place or chronological order, with interest in the names and biographies of most of those who came before Him, or with scene-painting for its own sake. In general, everything centres on a single point, and that a religious Gospel-point.

It will readily be seen how liable the method is to exaggeration and abuse. Some of its exponents indeed have tended to assume that any story or saying, which could conceivably have been applied in an apologetic or dogmatic interest, is as likely as not to have been created for the purpose, and probably therefore has no foundation in fact. The tendency to modify the narrative for particular purposes is undoubtedly present in the gospels, and was recognized long before form criticism was heard of; but there is no reason to think that it is present to a disconcerting degree, or to call in question the reliability of the record as a whole. Dr. B. S. Easton has shown in detail that we do not often find in the Lord's utterances during the ministry any clear traces of later developments. Thus it is well known how few are His references to the Holy Spirit, or to the Gentile mission. On the other hand, as regards those modifications which are certainly present, the new study shows for the first time in a clear light why they were made. The purpose was to reveal some Gospel-truth more clearly.

There is a widespread tendency in this country to value the gospels almost solely for what is believed to be their biographical worth, and concern is expressed if in any respect the books seem to fail to pass this standard. It may be said at once that, in the belief of those best entitled to express an opinion on the subject, the historical basis of Christianity, more essential to it than to any of the great religions of the world, is in no danger whatsoever and also that with the help of the gospels the main features of the Lord's character and teaching may become truly and well known to careful thought and study.* But the arguments by which it is sought to establish the historical reliability of the gospels are of varying value, and some of them probably will not bear all the weight which it is sometimes sought to place upon them. Thus very great emphasis is often laid upon the second-century tradition which connects St. Mark's gospel with St. Peter. Certainly there is reason to think that in some parts of his gospel St. Mark may well be giving us the latter's recollections. Passages among others in which this is especially likely to be the case are 1^{16-39}, 5^{21-43}, 9^{2-29}. But a close study of the book will suggest that in many parts of the book the tradition must be used with caution. Again, reference is often made to St. Luke's introduction 1^{1-4}, in support of the view that his purpose was simply to reproduce, in the words of a recent writer, 'the most primitive and authentic sources known to him'. Well, we have every reason to believe that one of the principal sources used by St. Luke was Mark, almost if not quite identical with the book which we have in our hands to-day. Let us then take one of the simplest and briefest sections of Mark, in which St. Peter himself plays a part, and let us consider St. Luke's treatment of it. We recall that St. Peter was the

---

* I take this opportunity to refer to a widespread misunderstanding of the last paragraph of the Bampton Lectures for 1934, in which I said that 'for all the inestimable value of the gospels, they yield us little more than a whisper of [the Lord's] voice; we trace in them but the outskirts of his ways'. This passage was frequently quoted in reviews and notices; but very few indeed of those who thus referred to it seemed to realize that it is almost a quotation from Job 26^{14}, to which unfortunately I omitted to give a reference, thinking that the allusion would be at once recognized and would also make clear in what way my words were to be understood. For the patriarch would have been even more grievously distressed than he already was, had he thought that his words would be taken to imply that he had practically no knowledge of his God. The last words of the verse, 'But the thunder of his power who can understand?' show that the point of the passage lies in the contrast between that comparatively small knowledge which in Job's view is all that is at present available to man, and the boundless immensity which is quite beyond his grasp.

leader of the Twelve, and we should naturally expect that St. Luke, *if* his chief purpose was that described above, namely, to reproduce unchanged the most primitive and authentic sources known to him, would treat a story, which he believed to be derived almost directly from the chief of the apostles, with scrupulous and undeviating accuracy. But this is hardly what we find to be the case. Let us place Mark 1³⁵⁻⁸ and its reproduction in Luke 4⁴² ᶠ· side by side, and compare the two passages. It may well be, as has been suggested, that St. Mark's narrative at this point is based, like other parts of Mark 1, ultimately on Petrine reminiscence; in any case, it is extremely lifelike. We infer from it that the Lord in the early morning, after a sabbath of strain and labour in Capernaum, found it imperative to go away and pray; and that Simon and his three associates (Mark 1¹⁶⁻²⁰· ²⁹), resentful that their Leader should neglect the door thus wonderfully opened, as they thought, at Capernaum, tracked Him down and remonstrated with Him.

But in Luke it is the crowds who go in search of Him, and on finding Him beg Him not to leave them. A strange rendering of the story, surely, on the part of St. Luke, *if* his purpose was to write 'plain history'. Can we then trace the motives which may have caused St. Luke to make the change, and can we thereby reconcile to some extent the apparent divergence between him and his authority? We notice, first, that it is a special characteristic of St. Luke to emphasize the nearness of the Lord to 'the crowds' or 'the people', and His great sympathy with them, and that in this gospel the people constantly welcome Him and give Him loyal support; and the present passage is the first example of this tendency on the part of this evangelist. Secondly, in the Marcan form of the story the four, in spite of Mark 1¹⁶⁻²⁰, do not act here as disciples, a word which does not occur in Mark till 2¹⁵, but as interpreters of the actions and wishes of others; 'all are seeking thee'. Hence, it may be only a slight step when St. Luke deletes them, as intermediaries between the people and the Lord, entirely, and brings the crowds themselves upon the scene.

If this exegesis of the passage is correct, the gulf between the two evangelists is not after all so great or so important as it may have seemed at first. None the less, with Mark before us, we are likely to feel that St. Luke's version deprives us of features of great value in the story; and certainly his version of it is not what we expect to-day from a writer of 'plain history'. And the consideration of this one example may have served to show how difficult and delicate are the problems which beset the student of the gospels; how cautious and patient he must be; and how resolutely he must decline to accept probabilities or possibilities as certainties.

Attention was invited, earlier in this chapter, to the *religious* significance seen by the new study in the various gospel sections. Whether the study will help us to draw nearer to the central Figure of the gospels, in His historical manifestation, we cannot say as yet; and in any case, as was pointed out above, form criticism had its origin in motives different from the hope which was the inspiration and driving force of source criticism, the hope, that is, of the recovery of 'plain biography'. Indeed, it came into existence largely through the failure of source criticism to realize this hope. We can, however, at least say that it is likely to increase our knowledge of the way in which the traditions of the ministry took shape in the earliest period, and to show that they probably assumed more or less definite forms some considerable time before they came into the hands of the evangelists. But the chief gain to religion from the new study will probably lie in a different direction. It will come through the emphasis of the new study on the vital connexion between the little sections, including the teaching, of the gospels and the great fundamental, permanent Gospel themes of vocation, physical and spiritual restoration, life and death, love and hate, judgement and salvation. It was probably to the light thrown by the historical traditions on these great themes, even more than to their historical interest, that the traditions themselves owed their preservation; and if form criticism can show once more the vital connexion in this respect between the gospels and the Gospel, it will have proved its value.

APPENDIX

In chapter 7 of this book it was maintained that St. Mark deliberately ended his gospel at 16^8. It is believed that the argument there set forth will be strengthened and perhaps in some points corrected,* if the possible implications of the remarkable references to Galilee in 14^{28} and 16^7 are considered more closely.†

In the Lord's last words in Mark to His disciples as a body, on their way after the last supper in the upper room to Gethsemane, He tells them 14^{27-31} that they will all lose confidence in Him, and that this is bound to happen, in accordance with scriptural prediction; but, He continues, 'after I am raised up, I will lead the way for you into Galilee'. This is the one and only ray of hope or comfort in the passage; for when Peter protests that he at least will not lose confidence, even if his loyalty should involve the sharing of his Master's death, he is explicitly assured that within a few hours he will repeatedly disown his Lord; and Peter's protestations of loyalty are echoed by all his colleagues.

The Lord's words are recorded to have been fulfilled to the letter; even before the Lord was escorted from Gethsemane, all the disciples had left Him and fled 14^{50}; and although Peter followed at a distance, the only result was his thrice repeated disownment of his Master. In Mark therefore the Lord in the closing scenes is left utterly alone, except that we read in $15^{40\ f.}$ of many women who watched from a distance the events at the cross. These women had followed the Lord about and attended to His wants in Galilee, and had gone up with Him to Jerusalem; and in 16^{1-8}, the concluding section of the book as I believe, three of these women come to the tomb early on the second day after the crucifixion in order to anoint the body, having been unable to carry out their intention on the previous day, because it was a sabbath. They learn, however, and indeed see for themselves, that the body is not there; and they are told that the first part of the Lord's words in 14^{28}, 'After I am raised up', have already been fulfilled. They are now bidden to go and tell His disciples that the fulfilment of the second half of His words in 14^{28}, 'I will lead the way for you into Galilee', is now taking place or, it may be, is about to do so; and the women are to add that there, in Galilee, He will be seen; and the book, as we have it, ends with a

* As also the argument in my previous book *Locality and Doctrine in the Gospels*, pp. 62–77.

† In this appendix I am indebted, for some of its leading ideas, to a remarkable sermon by Dr. T. W. Manson. He is, however, in no way responsible for the use which I have made of them here.

description of the flight of the women, utterly unnerved, from the tomb, and of their silence (even, it seems, in respect of the message with which they have been entrusted), due to fear.

Before we pass to consider the significance of these references to Galilee in 14²⁸ and 16⁷, it is desirable to emphasize two points. First, the discovery on the morning of the first day of the week that the Lord's body was not in the tomb where it had been laid on the Friday evening, however surprising, mysterious, and inexplicable, does not seem to have been regarded, except perhaps in a single, remarkable instance,* as, in itself, a convincing or sufficient demonstration of His risen life. The last chapter of St. Luke's gospel may be cited for explicit evidence of this. For there, in spite of verses 10 to 12, we find the hopes 24²¹ of the two disciples on their walk to Emmaus still shattered by their Master's death 24¹⁹ ᶠ·; and this, in spite of the verification of the reports of the women who had been early that morning at the tomb and had not found the body 24²²⁻⁴. It is only when the Lord personally makes Himself known to His fellow travellers that their amazement 24²² and heart-burning 24³² are resolved and that they find themselves driven to immediate action, in order to impart to others that which has just and for the first time become matter of knowledge and conviction to themselves 24³³; and having done so, they learn that they are not alone in their experience, since Peter shares it with them 24³⁴.

Secondly, certain passages in the conclusion of St. Luke's and St. John's gospels† suggest that it became increasingly important to emphasize the identity, in all respects, of the risen Lord, as the disciples now come increasingly to know Him, with the Master whom they had followed about in Galilee and had accompanied to Jerusalem. No doubt they know Him now in a less restricted, more compelling and mysterious, but also more satisfying way; but it was regarded as of vital importance to the truth of the Gospel that their risen Lord was no disembodied spirit Luke 24³⁷, but identical in every way with Him whose company they had shared in the days of His flesh. It may be for this reason that the risen Lord is represented Luke 24³⁸⁻⁴³ as drawing the attention of the disciples to the marks of the Passion in His hands and feet, and as eating before them (cf. Acts 1³ ᶠ· R.V. mg *bis* and 10⁴¹). Similarly in John 20¹⁶ the Lord becomes known to Mary Magdalene by His voice, and in 20²⁰ shows the ten disciples His hands and His side; and finally, although Thomas in spite of his earlier asseveration 20²⁵ does not in the end need to accept the Lord's invitation to him in 20²⁷ to satisfy himself,

---

* At John 20⁸ we read that the beloved disciple 'believed', on the evidence supplied to him by the emptiness of the tomb and the position of the gravecloths.

† In view of Matt. 28⁹, we may perhaps include St. Matthew's gospel also.

before he can believe, by tangible, physical proof that He is in touch with the same Master as of old, none the less the invitation is given.

The contents of the gospels in this respect should not surprise us; for to the Jewish mind resurrection implied full and complete restoration to the physical life and vigour previously enjoyed in this world. The doctrine of the immortality of the soul, widely held among the Greeks, or that of the survival of the spirit in some non-material sphere, would have seemed both disappointing and unsatisfying to Hebrew thought. Whatever changes may have taken place, resurrection must involve restoration to nation, family, and friends, recognition by them, and resumption, in some way, of the old activities. Thus we find Lazarus, after his resurrection, sitting at table, with his relatives round him, in his former home, John 12².

With these thoughts in mind, let us now review what we learn from St. Mark's gospel about Galilee, whither the Lord after His Passion, according to Mark 14²⁸ and 16⁷, will lead the way for His disciples; and since both sentences suggest that, in so doing, He will be especially concerned with His *disciples*, let us keep the disciples principally in view.*

Apart from the passages already mentioned (14²⁸, 15⁴¹, 16⁷), the word Galilee occurs nine times in Mark, and four of these occurrences are in the brief space of twenty-five verses† in the first chapter, 1¹⁴⁻³⁹. It was into Galilee, we read, that the Lord came, after John's activity was stopped, and uttered the momentous announcement and consequent requirement, which are summarized in 1¹⁵. At the outset two pairs of brothers are invited to join Him; but although they will in fact form the first third of the group of twelve, as appointed later, even the word disciple is not as yet applied to them. In the next two scenes 1²¹⁻⁷ and 1²⁹⁻³¹ the Lord and these four appear to form a single group 1²¹,²⁹ (although He and He only is the centre of interest in the incidents described, and indeed in 1³²⁻⁴ there is no mention of the four). On the following morning, however, the Lord finds it necessary to leave not only Capernaum but them, and to be alone for a time, if His work is to continue (see p. 23 f.); and when the four, now described as 'Simon and those with him', succeed in running Him down, they only reflect, all too closely, the wishes and action of those from whose insistent attentions the Lord has been

---

* At this point it becomes desirable, if the argument in this appendix is to be understood, to emphasize once more the warning, given on p. 83, against any attempt to conflate the contents of St. Mark's gospel with those of the other gospels.

† In the introduction to the gospel the Lord at 1⁹ comes from Nazareth, which is described as being 'of Galilee' and seems to be regarded as His native place, and undergoes the baptism of John in Jordan.

compelled to withdraw; to borrow a phrase used later in the book, at present they think 'like men, and not like God' 8³³. The Lord does not indeed reject them, but once more taking them with Him He begins an itinerant ministry throughout all Galilee (chiefly 1³⁹, though not exclusively 2¹³, in the synagogues), constantly changing the scene of His activities and teaching, of His work and word.

In chapter 2¹³ ᶠ· a revenue officer also joins the Lord; and we now hear also for the first time of disciples; it is said that there were many such, and that they were beginning to follow Him about, 2¹⁵; and complaint is made to them by the official classes about certain aspects of their Leader's conduct 2¹⁶. It is, however, the Lord who deals with the objections raised 2¹⁷, and also with the criticisms which the disciples themselves incur 2¹⁸·²⁴; the latter appear to play no active part. And we may perhaps assume that the evangelist wishes us to regard this state of affairs as continuing for some little time, the Lord acting (always with authority 1²²), and disciples in increasing numbers round Him, hearing His words, and seeing Him at work.

In chapter 3, however, a remarkable twofold event occurs. It seems that the synagogue ministry is over, owing to the opposition which it has aroused 3⁶; for the Lord is not found in Mark in the synagogue after 3¹⁻⁵, except for a single occasion 6¹⁻⁶, the significance of which will be considered later. Instead He withdraws, together with His disciples, to the open strand on the shore of the lake, to which He is followed by a great and pressing multitude from all those districts, in a wide area of the surrounding country, which were inhabited by Jews. Even in Capernaum, some time before, the thronging of the multitude would have made access to the Lord impossible for one who sorely needed His help in both soul and body, had it not been for most audacious and determined action on the part of his four friends 2⁴; and now the Lord finds it essential to put a distance between the crowd and Himself 3⁹, and also once more to silence utterances which drew attention to Himself 3¹¹ ᶠ·, cf. 1²⁴ ᶠ··.

Next, going up into the hills above the lake, the Lord calls certain men into His company, and they obey. Twelve are created, if we may use this word; and since the Lord's purpose in thus acting is explicitly stated 3¹⁴ ᶠ·, it will be well to dwell upon it. These twelve, some at least of whom seem to have already shared His company,* are to continue to do so, and thus to become fully acquainted with both His mind and method. But they are given this great privilege and opportunity not so much for their own advancement, as in order that they may be qualified to go out under His instructions and them-

---

* It should, however, be noticed that disciples *named as such* (perhaps contrast 1²¹⁻⁷) are not explicitly mentioned as being present at any single mighty act, narrated in detail, thus far.

selves to do the work, in both word and action, which He has been doing, hitherto alone; they are to declare* what He declared in chapter 1, and to have authority to restore men's health of mind and body; and as if to emphasize how great a change this new life will involve for them, the first three in the list of the twelve, which is now given, receive a fresh, new name, in addition to that by which they are already known; Simon for example becomes Simon man-of-granite.

It would probably be an error to regard the teaching of our second gospel as being or as intended to be altogether precise and definite either in respect of the order and precedence of the twelve among themselves or in respect of the exact relations between them and other disciples of the Lord. For as regards the order and precedence of the twelve among themselves, although on three occasions Peter, James, and John are taken by the Lord apart from the rest, yet on another private occasion Andrew, who was invited at the same time as these three to join the Lord, is found with them 13^3.† Again, although St. Peter is placed first here 3^{16} and is usually the foremost, both for good and ill, e.g. $8^{29.32}$, yet St. Mark's arrangement of his material on either side of the third proclamation of the Passion in chapter 10 may be intended to give further and different instruction on this subject. It is indeed often thought strange that whereas, after the first prediction of the Passion, Peter is outraged and rebukes his Master, and after the second prediction the disciples, we read, 'understood not the saying, and were afraid to ask him', at first sight there seems to be no similar reaction, or indeed reaction of any kind, after the third prediction, which is followed forthwith by the ambitious request of the sons of Zebedee. In making such a request at such a moment, they appear to be both blind to the picture painted in 10^{32} and deaf to the teaching given in 10^{33}. But possibly the difficulty will be found to disappear, if the context *on both sides of 10^{32-34}* is taken into account. In 10^{23-7}, after the decision against discipleship made by an aspirant who none the less aroused the Lord's affection 10^{21}, the Lord has been saying how difficult, indeed impossible but for divine help, is entry into the kingdom of God,

* This word, often, it seems, used in a technical sense for the proclamation of the Gospel, occurs three times in Mark 1 in reference to the Lord $1^{14.38.39}$, but not again after His contact with the leper 1^{40-5}. Elsewhere in Mark it is used of the Baptist 1^{4-7}, of the leper 1^{45}, of the disciples 3^{14}, 6^{12}, of the healed demoniac 5^{20}, and of those present at the restoration of a deaf and dumb 7^{32-7}.

† In the four lists of the twelve in the New Testament (Matt. 10^2, Mark 3^{16}, Luke 6^{14}, Acts 1^{13}) the names seem to fall into three groups of four, since each group is headed by the same name. But in no other respect is the order identical in all the four lists; and the place of Judas Iscariot, last in the first three lists, is vacant in the fourth.

and therewith salvation. Thereupon Peter points out 10^{28} that he and his colleagues (unlike the aspirant 10^{22}) have left all and followed Jesus. (St. Matthew, in his version 19^{27} of St. Peter's words here, adds 'What then shall we have?'; and the form of the Lord's reply in Mark suggests that the addition in Matthew correctly interprets the implication, a not entirely satisfactory implication, in St. Peter's words.) The Lord's reply ends with a warning that many will be last that were first, and first that were last; and this teaching is at once followed by the brief section 10^{32-4}, which describes the appearance of the company as it goes forward in its bewilderment, preceded by the Lord, towards Jerusalem, and finally the third and most explicit prediction of the Passion. Immediately after 10^{32-4}, we have the request of James and John, which is not only ambitious and therefore arouses the indignation of their colleagues 10^{41}, but also seems to exclude the leader Peter from the place of closest proximity to their common Master. The Lord's reply to the two disciples is as sympathetic and forbearing as that which He has already given to St. Peter; but it can hardly be doubted that all three disciples, and indeed the remaining nine also, are represented as having thus shown inability to understand their Lord; and the chapter ends, in contrast both to the aspirant of 10^{17-22} who has withdrawn, and to the twelve, with a description 10^{46-52} of the effect of the Lord's presence on one who has had no previous connexion with Him and indeed has hitherto, in his helplessness, been a prey upon society, but is now granted insight* sufficient to lead forthwith to enlightenment and consequent discipleship $10^{52\ \text{end}}$.

As regards the relations between the twelve and other disciples, it has just proved impossible, in our consideration of chapter 10 with reference to the order and precedence of the twelve among themselves, to keep other disciples entirely out of sight; and if we now return to chapter 4, we shall find the same conditions holding. The distinction between the disciples and the multitude has indeed become in chapter 4 even more clearly marked than it was in chapter 3. The crowd itself is now immense; nowhere else in this gospel is the superlative, here used, applied to it; and while it remains on the shore, the Lord at a slight distance, in a boat upon the water, instructs it by parables. But at 4^{10} (when the Lord is alone, apparently, so far as the crowd is concerned) a company is found with Him, described as 'they that were about him with the twelve'; and to this company, to which, we read (although it at present, no more than the crowd, understands the parabolic teaching), the

---

* The order of the words in the Greek, 'Son of David, Jesus', not, as in the R.V., 'Jesus, thou son of David', should especially be noticed.

mystery or secret of God's kingdom has been given, the Lord explains the parables and all else 4^{34b}, in expositions which it alone may have. It thus seems to be implied, first, that the Lord's teaching about His greatest theme, God's kingdom, must of necessity be symbolic in character 4^{34}, and secondly, that this teaching can only be received by those who have been divinely enlightened, or in the language of John 3^3 have been born anew (or, from above); but this enlightenment is by no means to be regarded as given only to the twelve. It is indeed often difficult to decide in a particular context, e.g. 6^1, 7^2, when the Lord's disciples are mentioned, whether only the twelve are in view, or a slightly larger body which includes the twelve. 'His disciples' in this gospel seems sometimes to be 'a general term describing those who were associated with him [the Lord] at any particular moment',* and sometimes, especially towards its close, to be a synonym for the twelve, e.g. 11^{11} when compared with 11^{14}, or 14^{12} when compared with 14^{17}.

According to St. Mark, it was on the evening of the day on which the twelve, with others,† had received the intimation of the special enlightenment granted to them, that at the Lord's suggestion, leaving the crowd, they cross the lake. It is remarkable that, when the storm arises, the disciples, some at least of whom were experienced fishermen 1^{16-20}, are not described as trying themselves to cope with the imminent danger; they apparently turn forthwith for assistance to Him who alone has no fear, since He is sleeping;‡ but even so, owing to the extremity of their fear, their words are not so much an appeal for help, as a reproach for seeming indifference. The Lord forthwith takes control of the situation, which is at once reduced to order; only the disciples, it appears, are still at fault; and as they had rebuked 4^{38}, so they are now rebuked 4^{40}. The combination (which occurs only here in Mark) of cowardice and want of faith is noteworthy. The disciples' cowardice was due to fear of shipwreck, although their Lord was with them in the boat; want of confidence is shown by their reproach of Him. Had they known who was with them 4^{41}, they could not have uttered the reproach of 4^{38}. As it is, however, they, like the women at the tomb 16^{1-8}, are left in the grip of extreme fear and lack of understanding or insight.

In 5^{2-34} the disciples play no part, except for their remark at 5^{31}; but in 5^{35-43}, when the Lord reveals Himself in His highest attribute as the vanquisher of death, three of the twelve are allowed to be

---

* C. H. Turner in *The Journal of Theological Studies*, Oct. 1926, p. 26.

† It seems possible that the reference in 4^{36} end to 'other boats' should be explained in the same way.

‡ This (with its parallels Matt. 8^{18-27}, Luke 8^{22-5}) is the only occasion in the gospels when the Lord is represented as sleeping.

present, along with the parents of the child. The teaching of the passage seems to be that the presence and action of the Lord imply the opposite of death (cf. John 11²⁵ ᶠ· ⁴³ ᶠ·), which in God's sight cannot be more than a sleep,* cf. 12²⁶ ᶠ·; hence the Lord's words in 5³⁹. The effect or result on those present is a great amazement.

It has already been mentioned that 6¹⁻⁶ is the only occasion after 3¹⁻⁶, when the Lord is found once more in the synagogue; and now, in His own country, it rejects Him.† St. Mark, and he only, expressly mentions that on this occasion the Lord's disciples followed Him 6¹; and the next section describes a new departure, the result, we may believe, of the rejection. For the first time the twelve are sent out, in six different companies, with His authority, and, as it might seem, in independence of Him, although it is His message which they are to give and His work which they are to do, cf. 1³⁸ ᶠ·. Their equipment is to be of the lightest 6⁸ ᶠ·, and the simplest hospitality is to suffice for them 6¹⁰; but, their message being what it is, they are to make clear that rejection of it involves extreme responsibility 6¹¹.

The reference to Herod Antipas in 6¹⁴, followed by the story of his earlier treatment of the Lord's forerunner John the Baptist 6¹⁷⁻²⁹, strongly suggests that the mission of the twelve has been recorded at this point, because the Lord knows that His own personal activities in Galilee are now almost over. As a whole, it has rejected Him‡ 6¹⁻⁶; and now the secular power has heard of Him, and will seek to deal with Him as it has already dealt with His forerunner. If His work is to be completed, it must be elsewhere than in Galilee. And in fact after chapter 6 and a final encounter with opponents in 7¹⁻²³ the Lord is not found again in Galilee in Mark except at a later date on His way through it to Jerusalem, a journey which by His wish 9³⁰ was to be kept a secret. The last two scenes in Galilee, however, call for careful notice.

When at 6³⁰ the twelve (who here and here only in Mark receive the title of apostles) return from their mission and report themselves

---

* The comparison of death and resurrection to falling asleep and awaking has strong Biblical support, e.g. Isa. 16¹⁹, Dan. 12², Matt. 27⁵², John 11¹¹, 1 Thess. 4¹³⁻¹⁵.

† It is unfortunate that the section Mark 6¹⁻⁶ is usually described as 'the rejection *at Nazareth*'. However true this may be, it is important to notice that the name of the *patris* is not given in Mark, and this, as I have tried to show elsewhere (*History and Interpretation in the Gospels*, ch. 7), is probably no accident. According to the point of view taken, the Lord's *patris* or *Heimat*, which rejects Him, may be regarded as Nazareth or Galilee or Jewry or, in Johannine language, the world.

‡ In the sense that it will not listen to and follow out His teaching, e.g. of repentance Mark 1¹⁵, and is therefore unable to receive that which He has come to bring Mark 1¹⁴. A rejection of this kind is not incompatible with the desire 'to take him by force, to make him king', John 6¹⁵.

to their Lord, He takes them apart with Him to a lonely place. He thus invites them to do as He did 1^{35}, after the crowded day in Capernaum. But just as on that occasion 1^{35-7} the four had tracked their Master down, so now the multitude breaks in upon the little company and frustrates the purpose which they had in view. And although, as we have learned, the multitude has rejected that which He has to give to it, and He knows that He must leave it, yet He finds Himself unable, as He sees its need of leadership and guidance, a need similar to that of lost sheep, Himself to reject it; and coming out He feeds it, both in mind 6^{34} and body 6^{42}, the distribution of the physical food being made by means of His disciples 6^{41}.

In the course of the section 6^{35-44} the disciples are represented as showing themselves little, if at all, better than the multitude in respect of an understanding of their Lord, and cf. 6^{52}; and the language of 6^{45} suggests that He sees an immediate separation between them and the multitude to be essential. If we may turn to John 6^{15} to find the reason for His action here, we learn there that after the recent event the multitude was becoming disposed to use violence, in order to force kingship on the Lord; and it was clear that their ideas of kingship were by no means His. The disciples therefore are peremptorily sent away by boat, and the multitude dismissed; and for some hours, it seems, the Lord is left alone. Meantime, however, the disciples in the absence of their Master are making little headway in their efforts to advance the boat; and the sight of their distress has the same effect as the sight of the multitude 6^{34} upon Him, and He must needs go to help them. None the less, such is the strain upon Him through their lack of comprehension and all that this implies and will involve, that just as He will pray later in Gethsemane that the hour might pass Him by 14^{35}, so now He would have been glad to pass them by $6^{48 \text{ end}}$ (the Greek verb is the same in the two passages);* and indeed when they see Him, they

---

* If this interpretation of 6^{48} end be thought possible, the question may be raised whether the position of the section on marriage and divorce 10^{1-12} cannot be satisfactorily explained along the same lines. The Lord has just arrived in the south, the sphere of hostility (3^{22}, 7^1) and the destined scene of His death. He is forthwith faced with the question whether a man may divorce his wife; and the last words of 10^2 show that the evangelist regarded the question as constituting a πειρασμός or temptation to Him.

The thought of Israel as the bride of Yahweh is familiar in the Old Testament, e.g. Isa. 50^1, $62^{4 \text{ f.}}$; and the Lord in Mark 2^{19} has spoken of Himself as a bridegroom. But by 10^{1-12} the reader has already learned, and not only in the two predictions of the Passion, that He will be rejected; and on the interpretation suggested the Lord finds Himself faced with the necessity of deciding whether at all costs to Himself He will maintain the union and remain faithful to His people, however they may treat Him. In this light the words 'What God hath joined together, let not man put asunder' 10^9 acquire very great significance.

one and all suppose that He is nothing better than a ghost, and cry out in their surprise and fear, which He vainly seeks to quell 6⁵⁰⁻².

Such then, according to this gospel, is in brief outline the story of the Lord's activities in Galilee, with special reference to His intercourse with the disciples. The story tells both of a great event Mark 1¹⁵—using modern terms, we might say that a new endowment is now declared to be possible for men—and of a great opportunity, which is, upon the whole, not taken. He who announces the event accompanies His teaching about it by a selfless ministry among the humble and the outcast, the sinful and the sick; and from the first He associates certain men of His choice to share in His ministry and teaching. They, however (as well as the populace generally, although the latter hangs upon His lips), are represented as failing signally to understand Him; and their failure is at least as strongly underlined as the hostility which He encounters, especially from the official classes of the capital 3²², 7¹, and seems to cause Him even more distress 4¹³·⁴⁰, 6³⁵⁻⁷, 7¹⁸, since to them He has sought to make clear the deeper meaning of His teaching; and it has been shown on p. 112 that this blindness, deafness, obtuseness, call it what we will, is represented as continuing throughout.* None the less, they continue to follow, even after the Lord not only has found it necessary to leave Galilee but is on His way to Jerusalem, with a full realization, we are given to understand, of the destiny which awaits the Son of man there; and in one of the most remarkable passages of the book we read of the company, as it were with halters round their necks 8³⁴, ascending to the capital, He Himself leading the way for them. Not until the arrest, after the three have failed to respond to their Master's request that they should share His vigil in Gethsemane 14³²⁻⁴², do they all desert Him, and He henceforth completes His work alone; and it is they, not He, by whom the unity is broken, 14⁴²ᵃ compared with 14⁵⁰.

The teaching of this gospel seems to be that nothing short of the Lord's death and resurrection, whereby He overcomes all resistance and is henceforth united indissolubly with His disciples, will enable them to understand Him† and to do His work. In and by themselves the disciples, to the end, are no better and have no more insight than the multitude. As the Lord feeds the multitude in chapter 6, so He must feed the disciples at the last supper in chapter 14; as the multitude misunderstands Him and His purpose in chapter 6, as interpreted by John 6¹⁵, so Peter misunderstands Him and His purpose in Gethsemane 14⁴⁷, again as interpreted by John 18¹⁰ ᶠ· But when the

---

* As also their inability to do His work; cf. 9¹⁸· ²⁸.

† This point is explicitly made in John 12¹⁶; cf. also John 2²², 13⁷.

Son of man has given Himself up and has been brought to nothing 9¹², then at length He in His fullness becomes theirs, and they His;* He no longer has any wish to withdraw from them 1³⁵ or to pass them by 6⁴⁸, nor is it necessary for Him any more to rebuke their lack of understanding, if they will but yield themselves to Him and to the enlightenment offered by Him for the work to which He calls them. And that work is His work, the salvation of the world, represented in the earlier chapters of this gospel by the multitude in Galilee.

If this interpretation of our second gospel is correct, the great importance and significance of the reference to Galilee in 14²⁸ and 17⁷ become apparent. For there the disciples have a work awaiting them, and in it their Lord will still lead the way for them, as He did before; what He did, when He was with them, He will still do in and through their work for Him; but, thanks to His self-oblation for their sakes (cf. John 17¹⁹), they are now to be enabled to see Him as He is, their Lord, and therefore to do His work, no longer blindly, but with sight and understanding, and, above all, with authority and power. Thus in the reference to Galilee in the Lord's last words to His disciples 14²⁸, which are taken up afresh in 16⁷, the reader's thought is turned back to the story of the ministry in the early chapters of the book, and he perceives that this is also the ministry to be fulfilled henceforth by the Lord (Himself no longer hampered or restricted, as in the days of His flesh) in and through His disciples, who now represent Him in the world. The reader is thus enabled to discern both the task and the message† of the church of which he is a member, and the book is seen to be complete.‡

* See the remarks on resurrection, p. 109, and cf. Gal. 2²⁰.

† No doubt the message is now greatly enlarged and intensified owing to the completion and perfecting of their Master's work; but it is still in essentials the same task and the same message, informed by the same spirit and directed to the same end.

‡ It should be borne in mind that, whatever conclusion may be reached about the original ending of St. Mark's gospel, verses 9 to 20 in ch. 16 are part of the canonical scriptures, accepted in and by the universal Church. Dr. Hort (*The New Testament in the Original Greek*, vol. 2, 'Notes on Select Readings, 36) thus points out their importance. 'They contain', he says, '(1) a distinctive narrative, one out of four, of the events after the day of the Resurrection; (2) one of the (at most) three narratives of the Ascension; (3) the only statement in the Gospels historical in form as to the Session at the Right Hand; (4) one of the most emphatic statements in the New Testament as to the necessity of faith or belief; and (5) the most emphatic statement in the New Testament as to the necessity of baptism.'

INDEX

PRINTED IN
GREAT BRITAIN
AT THE
UNIVERSITY PRESS
OXFORD
BY
CHARLES BATEY
PRINTER
TO THE
UNIVERSITY